First World War
and Army of Occupation
War Diary
France, Belgium and Germany

50 DIVISION
Headquarters, Branches and Services
Commander Royal Engineers
16 April 1915 - 31 May 1916

WO95/2816/1

The Naval & Military Press Ltd
www.nmarchive.com
Published in association with The National Archives

Published by

The Naval & Military Press Ltd

Unit 10 Ridgewood Industrial Park,

Uckfield, East Sussex,

TN22 5QE England

Tel: +44 (0) 1825 749494

www.naval-military-press.com

www.nmarchive.com

This diary has been reprinted in facsimile from the original. Any imperfections are inevitably reproduced and the quality may fall short of modern type and cartographic standards.

© **Crown Copyright**
Images reproduced by permission of The National Archives, London, England, 2015.

Contents

Document type	Place/Title	Date From	Date To
Heading	WO95/2816/1		
Heading	C.R.E. Apr 1915-May 1919		
Heading	War Diary Of 50th Northumbrian Divisional Royal Engineers From 16/4/15 to 31/5/15 Volume I		
War Diary	Nawcastle	16/04/1915	16/04/1915
War Diary	Southampton	17/04/1915	17/04/1915
War Diary	Havre	18/04/1915	18/04/1915
War Diary	Hazebruck	19/04/1915	20/04/1915
War Diary	Steenvoorde	20/04/1915	12/05/1915
War Diary	Poperinghe	15/05/1915	25/05/1915
War Diary	Watou	26/05/1915	31/05/1915
Heading	War Diary of C.R.E. 50th (Northn) Divl RE From-2nd June 1915 To 30th June 1915		
War Diary	L19b Sheet 27	02/06/1915	04/06/1915
War Diary	G 27b Sheet 28	05/06/1915	24/06/1915
War Diary	St Jans Cappel	25/06/1915	30/06/1915
Heading	War Diary Of 50th (Northn) Divisional R.E. From 1st July to 31st July 1915 (Volume III)		
Heading	Diary Of C R E 50th Division For July 1915		
War Diary	St Jans Cappel	01/07/1915	20/07/1915
War Diary	Armentieres	21/07/1915	31/07/1915
Heading	Hdqrs R E 50th Division Vol IV		
Miscellaneous		31/08/1915	31/08/1915
War Diary	Armentieres	01/08/1915	31/08/1915
Heading	Hdqrs R.E. 50th Division Vol V		
Heading	War Diary of C.R.E. 50th Division of September 1915		
War Diary	Armentieres	01/09/1915	30/09/1915
Heading	Hdqrs R.E. 50th Division Vol VI		
Heading	War Diary C.R.E. 50th Division From 1/10/15 to 31/10/15		
War Diary	Armentieres	01/10/1915	31/10/1915
Heading	H.Q. R.E 50th Div Nov Vol VII		
Heading	War Diary of C.R.E. 50th Division 1st-30th November 1915		
War Diary	Armentieres	01/11/1915	02/12/1915
Heading	War Diary Of C.R.E. 50th Division From 1/12/15-31/12/15		
War Diary	Armentieres	01/12/1915	06/12/1915
War Diary	Caestre	07/12/1915	14/12/1915
War Diary	Reninghelst	15/12/1915	16/12/1915
War Diary	Farm 1 1/2 Miles on Poperinghe-Reninghelst Road	17/12/1915	31/12/1915
Heading	H.Q. R.E. 50th Div Jan Vol IX		
War Diary	Farm 1 1/2 Miles on Poperinghe Reninghelst Road	01/01/1916	25/01/1916
War Diary	Billet 1 1/2 Miles On Poperinghe Reninghelst Road	26/01/1916	30/01/1916
War Diary	Farm 1/2 Miles On Reninghelst Poperinghe Road	31/01/1916	31/01/1916
Heading	War Diary C.R.E. 50th Division From Feb 1st 1916 To Feb 29th 1916		
War Diary	Farm 1 1/2 Miles On Reninghelst Poperinghe Road	01/02/1916	04/02/1916
War Diary	Farm 1 1/2 Miles On Poperinghe Reninghelst Road	05/02/1916	09/02/1916

War Diary	Farm 1 1/2 Miles N If Reninghelst T G.27.c.01 Poperinghe Road	10/02/1916	20/02/1916
War Diary	Farm 1 1/2 Miles N If Reninghelst G.27.b.	21/02/1916	26/02/1916
War Diary	Farm A.27.b. On Reninghelst. Poperinghe Road	27/02/1916	29/02/1916
Heading	War Diary Of C.R.E. 50th Division From 1st March 1916 To 31st March 1916		
War Diary	Farm At G.15.b. on Reninghelst Poperinghe Road	01/03/1916	14/03/1916
War Diary	Farm At G.15.b.Sheet 28. on Reninghelst Poperinghe Road	15/03/1916	29/03/1916
War Diary	Farm At G.15.b. on Reninghelst Poperinghe Road	30/03/1916	31/03/1916
Heading	War Diary Of C.R.E. 50 Division From 1st April 1916 To 30th April 1916		
War Diary	Farm G.27.b. Reninghelst Poperinghe	01/04/1916	01/04/1916
War Diary	Westoutre	02/04/1916	24/04/1916
War Diary	Fletre	25/04/1916	30/04/1916
Heading	War Diary Of C.R.E. 50th Division From 1st May 1916 To 31st May 1916		
War Diary	Fletre	01/05/1916	26/05/1916
War Diary	Westoutre	27/05/1916	31/05/1916

WD 95/2816/1

50TH DIVISION

C. R. E.
APR 1915-MAY 1 919

Confidential

War Diary
of
50th (Northumbrian)
Divisional
Royal Engineers

From 16/4/15 to 21/5/15

Volume I

WAR DIARY
or
INTELLIGENCE SUMMARY.
(Erase heading not required.)

Army Form C. 2118.

C.R.E. 50th (NORTHUMBRIAN) Division

Place	Date	Hour	Summary of Events and Information	Remarks and references to Appendices
NEWCASTLE	16/4/15	2.30pm	Head Quarters NORTHUMBRIAN DIVISIONAL ROYAL ENGINEERS entrained. MM	
SOUTHAMPTON	17/4/15	4.0am	Arrived. MM	
do	do	8.30pm	Embarked on board HMT "AFRICAN PRINCE" MM	
HAVRE	18/4/15	10.30am	Arrived & disembarked	
do	do	11.30pm	Entrained & left HAVRE MM	
HAZEBROUCK	19/4/15	7.30pm	Detrained. Billeted for the night. Proceed to STEENVOORDE in morning. MM	
do	20/4/15	10.30am	Left HAZEBROUCK	
STEENVOORDE	do	11.15am	Arrived & went into billets MM	
do	20/4/15	9.0pm	2nd Field Coy WINNEZEELE district with 2nd Field Coy NORTHUMBRIAN DIV: R.E. MM	
do	21/4/15		2nd FIELD Coy N.D.R.E. moved to join NORTHUMBERLAND BDE & marched to meet in the via WINNEZEELE - DROGLANDT - WATOU. Left 2nd F.C. N.D.RE. at DROGLANDT & reported to BRIG. GEN. RIDDELL. Capt. J.A. McQUEEN R.E. ADJUTANT accompanied 2nd F.C. with recommendation of H.Q. Div. at C.R.E's recommendation. MM	

Army Form C. 2118.

WAR DIARY
INTELLIGENCE SUMMARY.
(Erase heading not required.)

C.R.E. 50th (NORTHUMBRIAN) DIVISION

Place	Date	Hour	Summary of Events and Information	Remarks and references to Appendices
STEENVOORDE	24/4/15	10 am	2 Officers & 182 O.R. of FRENCH ARMY reported for road-making pm	
do	26/4/15		108 of above detailed for police duty towards ST. SYLVESTRE – CAPPEL – WINNEZEELE – WATOU – ABEELE. Remainder (74) put to work on road STEENVOORDE – ABEELE as far as the BELGIAN FRONTIER pm	
do	4/5/15	9 am	2nd Fd Co. N.D.R.E. ordered to return from Burgomme 1 mile east of VLAMERTINGHE to STEENVOORDE, moving after dark via POPERINGHE – ABEELE. pm	
do	5/5/15	9 am	2nd Fd Co N.D.R.E. arrived & went into billets pm	
do	6/5/15	10 am	French road-makers put to work on repair of road STEENVOORDE – WATOU road as far as BELGIAN FRONTIER pm	
—	7/5/15	9 am	French road-makers ordered to commence work in repair of road STEENVOORDE – ST. SYLVESTRE – CAPPEL as soon as men available pm	
do	9/5/15	12 noon	Orders received for 2nd Field Co. N.D.R.E to move at 3.15 pm to BRANDHOEK via POPERINGHE pm	
do	do	3.15 pm	2nd Fd Co N.D.R.E. left for BRANDHOEK under the command of	

3

Army Form C. 2118.

WAR DIARY
or
INTELLIGENCE SUMMARY.
(Erase heading not required.)   C.R.E. 50th (NORTHUMBRIAN) DIVISION

Instructions regarding War Diaries and Intelligence Summaries are contained in F. S. Regs., Part II. and the Staff Manual respectively. Title pages will be prepared in manuscript.

Place	Date	Hour	Summary of Events and Information	Remarks and references to Appendices
STEENVOORDE	4/7/15	3.15pm	Captain J. McQueen R.E. Jnr. ordered to proceed to POPERINGHE via ABEELE. Left STEENVOORDE at 10.15 a.m. and arrived POPERINGHE 12.15 p.m. & went into billets.	
do	4/5/15	9.45am	From 33 and all R.E. man were busy cleaning and aired at STEENVOORDE. Two men of 2nd July A left with R.E. Gen Jnr for this purpose. Jnr	
POPERINGHE	5/7/15		Visited O.C. Durham L.I. 6 Durham L.I. Dee Jnr ETANGE DE ZILLEBEKE Sheet 28 I 22 Al & POTIJZE I 4 L. The trenches are in a very bad state. Trenches in rear with dugouts require F.C. works but no R.E. available. Took 2 & 2nd field Cos to inspect it & 84 Infantry. Told they cannot be spared from present work. Jnr	
do	6/7/15 2pm		Reorganise R.E. 750 accompanied Jnr Col G. 50 FLUSH Bn in Jeffrey of Northumbrian Div & left reconnoitred new Jossary billets Jnm York Rd near AC Company Cathedral R.W. Ry Crossing & POPERINGHE. Also found 2 directed C.R.E. Jnr	

1577 Wt. W10791/1773 500,000 1/15 D. D. & L. A.D.S.S./Forms/C. 2118.

WAR DIARY
or
INTELLIGENCE SUMMARY. C R.E. 50TH (NORTHUMBRIAN) DIVISION

(Erase heading not required.)

Instructions regarding War Diaries and Intelligence Summaries are contained in F.S. Regs., Part II. and the Staff Manual respectively. Title pages will be prepared in manuscript.

Place	Date	Hour	Summary of Events and Information	Remarks and references to Appendices
POPERINGHE	21/5/15	3.0 pm	Under instructions from 50th Division Hd.Qrs moved Divisional R.E. Park, that one wagon A.S.C. army to billet being in the area regular, subject to the supply from Mount Tir Watou & went into billets there	
do	25/5/15	10 am	Ordered to move to ABEELE & see CHIEF ENGINEER 5TH CORPS with a view of forming advanced DIVISIONAL R.E. PARK. He stated this could not be done until the road, which down by the 50TH (NORTHUMBRIAN) DIVISION had been decided on. Reverted that of minimum stores to be kept in park when formed.	
do	26/5/15	11 am	Casualty. The horse of Capt R.W. SIMPSON R.A.M.C. fell with him [near H.18.a SHEET 2] in nearly kicked him in the jaw breaking his jaw. He was evacuated to [2nd FIELD AMBULANCE & sent to] MT DE CAT HOSPITAL.	
do	30/5/15	10 pm	Received instructions to erect huts fr G.H.Q + AAQMG 50TH DIVISION or farm situated in L19.b + L13.d SHEET 2). Drew material for 3 CORPS R.E. PARK & commenced work 1pm	

Army Form C. 2118.

WAR DIARY
or
INTELLIGENCE SUMMARY.

(Erase heading not required.) C.R.E. 50TH (NORTHUMBRIAN) DIVISION

Instructions regarding War Diaries and Intelligence Summaries are contained in F. S. Regs., Part II. and the Staff Manual respectively. Title pages will be prepared in manuscript.

Place	Date	Hour	Summary of Events and Information	Remarks and references to Appendices
WATOU	3/5/15	8.0 am	Work continued in huts for Division. Received notice to move re 19d & 13d Sheet 2) at 11.0 am. Moved to 50th (Northumbrian) Division RE at 2.30 pm.	

R. M. Phan
Bt. Col. R.E. (T.)
C.R.E. 50th (North) Div.

3/5/15

1577 Wt. W10791/1773 500,000 1/15 D. D. & L. A.D.S.S./Forms/C. 2118.

50th Division

Confidential   121/5871

War Diary
of
C.R.E.
50th (North'n) Div'n R.E.

From:- 2nd June 1915

To:- 30th June 1915

(Volume II)

Army Form C. 2118.

WAR DIARY
INTELLIGENCE SUMMARY.
(Erase heading not required.)

C.R.E. 50TH (NORTHUMBERIAN) Division

Instructions regarding War Diaries and Intelligence Summaries are contained in F.S. Regs., Part II. and the Staff Manual respectively. Title pages will be prepared in manuscript.

Place	Date	Hour	Summary of Events and Information	Remarks and references to Appendices
L19.d. Sheet 28	26/5/15	10 am	Proceeded with Major BONHAM-CARTER to KRUISSTRAAT SHEET 28 H18.d. & district to settle advanced post for Divisional Hd Qrs. Decided to make slight extension advanced at LA TINNE N.W. KRUISSTRAAT. 10 pm Capt J.A. MCQUEEN R.E. reported Divisional R.E. Hd Qrs having been relieved in the Command of the 2nd Fd Co. N.D.R.E. by Capt E.C. BURNUP from the 1st Fd Co. N.D.R.E. Have been informed unofficially that the 1st & 2nd Fd Co N.D.R.E. are now attached to the 50th Div from 2nd Duns (evening) — Casualty. 1st Lt T. FOSTER 2nd Fd Co N.D.R.E. slightly wounded. on duty. R.E.	
to H Qrs	3/6/15	9.00 am	Accompanied by Adjutant (Capt J.A. MCQUEEN R.E.) visited the two Field Cos & arranged billets for them in the new area allotted to 5th Div. Arranged with CHIEF ENGINEER 5th CORPS to take over advanced R.E. Park later used by the 27th DIV near VLAMERTINGHE & 50th Div advanced park. Arranged to make a further advanced park at KRUISSTRAAT. The advanced post for 50th DIV Hd. Qrs will be commenced on 4/6 by the 1st Fd Co N.D.R.E. Ordered to move in	

1577 Wt. W10791/1773 500,000 1/15 D. D. & L. A.D.S.S./Forms/C. 2118.

WAR DIARY
INTELLIGENCE SUMMARY.

Army Form C. 2118.

(Erase heading not required.) C.R.E. 50th (NORTHUMBRIAN) DIVISION

Place	Date	Hour	Summary of Events and Information	Remarks and references to Appendices
L19b Sheet 28	3/6/15	am	on arriving I G 27 b 7 NE near BUSSEBOON Sheet 28	
	4/6/15	9.30	moved Hd Qrs 50th Div R.E. to G 27 b & went under canvas having office & farm house. Received orders to meet G.S.O.1 at 10 am to go over ground lines taken over by 50th Div	
G 27 b Sheet 28	5/6/15	10 am	Left in motor with Major HORDERN G.S.O.1 + Capt J.A. McQUEEN R.E. ADJUTANT to maplet trenches. Were joined in YPRES by BRIGADE MAJOR IXth BRIGADE + Capt L.C. BURNUP commanding 2/1st DNDRE + examined Trenches I 30 C T 1 24 d + G.H.Q. trenches ZILLEBEKE - TUILERIE describing what work was required. Returned to KRUISSTRAAT + saw dug-outs being built for Div H.Q.R.s advanced hut.	
do	do	2 pm	Attended with Adjutant conference at Hd Qrs 50th Div with reference to taking over above trenches L. 14.9th 153rd - 151st Bns on 6/7 June. 7 am	
do	7/6/15	4:45 pm	Proceeded by motor with ADJUTANT to KRUISSTAAT + were joined there by Capt E.C. BURNUP O.C. 2nd ½ol DNDRE examined G.H.Q. line from I.30.a 7.8. & ZILLEBEKE, a working party of 2 sections of 2nd DNDRE under 2/Lt T. FORSTER and G.M. HUME with a working party of 200 7th D.L.I.	

Army Form C. 2118.

WAR DIARY
INTELLIGENCE SUMMARY.
(Erase heading not required.) C.R.E. 50th (NORTHUMBRIAN) DIVISION

Instructions regarding War Diaries and Intelligence Summaries are contained in F.S. Regs., Part II. and the Staff Manual respectively. Title pages will be prepared in manuscript.

Place	Date	Hour	Summary of Events and Information	Remarks and references to Appendices
G 27 b SHEET 28	7/5/15		men engaged repairing trench 200 yards south from 116 d. Examined TUILERIE & decided myself required to place some in state of defence.	
do	8/5/15	6.30 AM	Attended conference at H.Q.50 & explained work to be carried out. Was left to write for front line trenches calling for O.C. 2nd Fd. C.N.D.R.E. at the Billet H 21 B. Left with H 21 B.	
do	9/5/15	10 AM	Left with men to front line trenches calling for O.C. 2nd Fd. C.N.D.R.E. 150th BDE at ECOLE DE BIENFAISANCE with reference to working by day in MAPLE COPSE I 23 L d. and SANCTUARY WOOD I 24 S d. Aeroplane report that large working parties can be seen during day. Permission given for small parties to work provided cover is taken up the appearance of aeroplane. Accompanied by Capt. Guy. BDE MAJOR 150 BDE examined work in MAPLE COPSE which is being put in a state of defence all round and all round defence point C 1 at N.W. corner of COPSE. Left Capt. Guy in SANCTUARY WOOD & was joined by H.H. L.H. DOUGLAS and O.D.CASE who are staffing these with wire entanglement of C.N.D.R.E. examined trenches & retrenchment of position in 130 C pointing out various work to be carried out. Interviewed O.C. 171st Co. R.E. Attachment tunnelling at this point. Was informed that the enemy were heard	

1577 Wt.W10791/1773 500,000 1/15 D. D. & L. A.D.S.S./Forms/C. 2118.

WAR DIARY

INTELLIGENCE SUMMARY.

(Erase heading not required.) C.R.E. 50TH (NORTHUMBRIAN) DIVISION

Army Form C. 2118.

Place	Date	Hour	Summary of Events and Information	Remarks and references to Appendices
G 27 b SHEET 28	9/6/15		enemy towards us on the 5th inst. That a charge of 180 lbs Ammonal was fired about 1.0 A.M on 6th inst. Dispelled to make this a defensive work with a tunnel 180 ft to the left and 80 feet right from tunnel head with listening points. On return pointed out to Capt Burnup a place & screen T/23 a.c. about 10 yards and a communication trench to be made from the S.E. end of ETANG DE ZILLEBEKE T/22 a 3.7. Both places being regularly sniped by the enemy.	
do		11.30 am	Capt J.A. McQUEEN R.E. ADJUTANT accompanied BRIG GEN JUDWINE G.S.O. 1 5TH CORPS, Brig Gen PETRIE C.E. 5TH CORPS and Lt Col HORDERN G.S.O. 1 50TH DIV T ZILLEBEKE to go over the defences which have to be undertaken by the 50th Div. The TUILERIE & G.H.Q Line as far as POTIGE was also examined & work decided on.	
do		6.30 pm	Attended conference at Hdqrs & explained work being carried on &c.	
do	10/6/15	11 am	Received note that 149th Inf Bde was to take over line now held by 7th Bde of 3rd Divn on night of 14/15 June. Instructed to see C.R.E. 3rd Div about details of work now in hand on that line & their arrangements.	

Army Form C. 2118.

WAR DIARY
or
INTELLIGENCE SUMMARY.

(Erase heading not required.) C.R.E. 50th (NORTHUMBRIAN) DIVISION.

Hour, Date, Place	Summary of Events and Information	Remarks and references to Appendices
10/5/15 G.27.b SHEET 28	C.R.E. 3rd Div. out when I called. Went	
	Adjutant later & he promised to call at 6 p.m.	
	Arranged with tracing parties to work	
	C.O.W.	
	C.W.S. WILSON C.R.E. 3rd Div. called & handed	
	me tracing & details of work required on working	
	on the FRASCATI-HOOGE line. 3 sections would	
	work at night supplying the working parties	
	which occupy ST ANDRE. 2 sections of ½	
	our own 4 Coys. 28th Div. would find	
	our own + small working party. The sappers	
	and spoil would remain in night dugouts.	
	The sections are now	
	based in FELIX. 3 on SANCTUARY WOOD	
	2 on ... the HOOGE line B.C.13.D.C.	
	on SHEET 27 & H.21 & SHEET 28 working on GHQ	
	may blind ZILLEBEKE	
	arranged that 1/5 A.R.E. in L. Coy with	
	BNL + ½ NR 1/5 NO C.R. on huts Coy managing	
	CHEMICAL SECTION (LT. ROBERTSON)	

Army Form C. 2118.

WAR DIARY
or
INTELLIGENCE SUMMARY.
(Erase heading not required.) C.R.E. 50TH DIVISION

Hour, Date, Place	Summary of Events and Information	Remarks and references to Appendices
1/6/15 — G 27.6 SHEET 28 2.30 pm 12/6/15 ab	E Div R.E. HQrs. FIELD TROOP S.M attached for work. O.C. CAPT MORIN reported. Instructed him to construct strong point at I 34 B 2.8 SHEET 28 commencing following night. Pm proceeded with ADJUTANT to Hd Qrs 149 Bde & arranged for entering parties to be detailed from the Bde in SANCTUARY WOOD for work in trenches at or near HOOGE. Saw O.C. 2 Nd. C. N.D.R.E. 'gave him full particulars.	
7.0 am. 13/6/15	The ADJUTANT proceeded to see O.C. 2 Nd. C.N.D.R.E. to make fresh arrangements & section 1 Plt Lieut GRAHAM E killed in action about midnight. Two sections have now placed 3 sections in line from I 2 and It. HOOGE. Lieut T. FORSTER has been sent up to take the place of Lieut HUME (killed) I section 2nd 2nd C.N.D.R.E. under Lieut C.I. BURRELL has been ordered to take on the work at 1.30 C in place of I Plt. DOUGLAS who has been sent to the HOOGE trenches. Instructed Lieut R. GIBSON to proceed with communication trenches on east side of ETANG DE ZILLEBEKE with I Lt T. FORSTERS section. Sent ADJUTANT and O.C. 2 Nd C.N.D.R.E.

Army Form C. 2118.

WAR DIARY
or
INTELLIGENCE SUMMARY.
(Erase heading not required.) CRE 37TH DIVISION

Instructions regarding War Diaries and Intelligence Summaries are contained in F.S. Regs., Part II. and the Staff Manual respectively. Title pages will be prepared in manuscript.

Hour, Date, Place	Summary of Events and Information	Remarks and references to Appendices
2.0 pm 13.6.15 G27 b SHEET 28	See report on Trenches around HOOGE. Report received that trenches are in bad state, all arrangements made to have them made good.	
9.30 am 14.6.15 do	Accompanied GENERAL LINDSAY & G.S.O.1 to HQ 9th & 14th Bde YPRES with reference to work being carried on near HOOGE.	
9.0 am 15.6.15 do	Attended conference at Divisional HQrs with reference to attack on night of 15/16 June from HOOGE on left.	
2.30 pm do	Accompanied by ADJUTANT met 2nd Lt [?] 149th Bde HQrs with officer & Sapper work & working parties. Instructed to carry on as ordered up to tonight. Instructed when affair opens on to take midnight SANCTUARY WOOD & clear of KRUISTRAAT village. Called at HQ of 2nd LONDRES & gave all necessary orders to O.C. Company. On return Earl Staff conveyed that he did not obtain command in SANCTUARY WOOD to cover this should be required. Orders sent to O.C. 2nd L to this effect. B/Lt T. FORSTER and [?] known with it a [?] [?] Trench line around HOUSE. From 1 pm.	

WAR DIARY
INTELLIGENCE SUMMARY.
(Erase heading not required.) **C.R.E. 50th DIVISION**

Army Form C. 2118.

Hour, Date, Place	Summary of Events and Information	Remarks and references to Appendices
12.15 a.m. 16.6.15 G.27.b SHEET 28.	Telegram dated 15th 2.45 p.m received from OC 1/1 K.O. R.E. HOOGE stating he could have energetic working under the parapet of BULL FARM trench to make them more...[illegible]... shallow. He has applied to OC BORDER REG.T. [illegible] would copy to OC 2nd field Co R.E. TERDEGHEM. There are no working parties available for tonight. [illegible]	
2.45 a.m. 17.6.15 G.27.b SHEET 29	Instructions received of forced ADVANCED DIV.N HDQRS KRUISSTRAAT as soon as possible	
8.30 a.m. do.	A C.J. sappers + working parties arranged for [illegible] around HOOGE. Captain J. 2nd field Co R.E. reported his company ...[illegible]... from 50th DIV.N Bill [illegible] for [illegible] in H.13.c SHEET 28.	
9.0 a.m. 16.6.15 do.	Ordered 1st [illegible] Co R.D.R.E. to return to billet in H.21.b in 18.E. 1 section to be sent up from last [illegible] and company tonight. 7.30 pm C. R.E. went with [illegible] in H.20.a.g.g. 9 pm [illegible] Lemon + OC 2 Field C. R.E. reported. Arranged that his company should start work in ZILLEBEKE	

13.

WAR DIARY
INTELLIGENCE SUMMARY
(Erase heading not required.) C.R.E. 50TH DIVISION

Army Form C. 2118.

Hour, Date, Place	Summary of Events and Information	Remarks and references to Appendices
9.0 a.m. 10.6.15. G.5.6 Sheet 28	Portion of the line called at HdQrs of Div. Saw G.S.O.1 with reference to work required of THODGE. Rine line to be pushed up by sapping & several tunnel dugouts on south of MENIN ROAD to shelter men near mouth. The ADJUTANT Capt. VAUGHREN R.E. provided & HOOGE accompanied by Capt. E.C. BURNUP Capt. ANDRE & inspected work at it. Trench E Left C.O. CASE reports support trench on left of trench 1300 yards in front of dugout completed about 1 ft of LEFT C. MAPLE Copse made. Captain Livingston left shortly. I saw report of leg order in Junction Sheet RIGHT CASE plan on them made good. Communication trench in east end of ZILLEKENE LAKE widened & deepened to 1th village few LAKE improved and given to fast one. Bridge over new stream. Total dugouts of commn. trench 900 yards. Capt. McQUEEN reports that sapping is	

WAR DIARY
or
INTELLIGENCE SUMMARY.
(Erase heading not required.) ORE 50TH DIVISION

Army Form C. 2118.

Hour, Date, Place	Summary of Events and Information	Remarks and references to Appendices
16.6.15 G.S.) SHEET 21	Being carried at HOOGE continuously from 11th both round STABLES & a barricade of 1000 sandbags placed west well leading to also being brought in truck on south of MENIN ROAD. Operation order No. 2 by 60TH DIVISION received on night 18/19th. From op. Bn of 3rd Div. will take over the front line on night of 19/20 TH Div to meet east of HOOGE village about H.16.674 from H.9.7.69.71. On night 19/20 2 Bns. numbers of 147th Bde 49th Div. Side on p. 2 of 9.9 and be taken over by 151st Bde. 13th. On completion of relief on night 19/20 the 49th June the disturbing lines between 3rd and 49th Divisions will be from point of junction with present line (1 of 9.9) to road junction H.4.9.2.5 thence westwards until of turnip in H.23.9 and a central to road junction H.16.d.2.2 thence to south of point where the ZILLEBEKE SWITCH line crosses the ridge in H.16.d.3.4 thence west of that road & of farm to H.15.c.6.6 thence eastwards to H.15.c.0.10 of westwards until junction with 2 hedges 13 about H.15.8.1.7.3 a 8.3 westerly of CANAL LINE	

15.

Army Form C. 2118.

16

WAR DIARY
or
INTELLIGENCE SUMMARY.
(Erase heading not required.) C.R.E. 50TH DIVISION

Instructions regarding War Diaries and Intelligence Summaries are contained in F.S. Regs., Part II. and the Staff Manual respectively. Title pages will be prepared in manuscript.

Hour, Date, Place	Summary of Events and Information	Remarks and references to Appendices
10.6.15 G.2.J.6 SHEET 28	The requirements for holiday arrangements for Brigade 14 & remain with 50th Div. from this competition began in night 18/19 detachment 1/5th FC and RE transferred to 3rd Div.	
7.30 a.m. 19/6/15 G.2.J.6 SHEET 28	Copy received of confidential letter from General Staff 20th Divn dated 18th June 1915 and 5.62 & Divn as follows — "Johnhill he much obliged if you would convey to Major Pollard D.S.O. and all ranks of the 1/1st Northumbrian Field Company R.E. my regret at not having been able to see the company and thank them personally for the good work they did whilst under my command. The confidence of my and the 26th Division at Winchester and afterwards that time unto they were sent to you the 50th Division all ranks have invariably got not often enough over saying and conforming in letters for the company and of the soldiers, and to appreciation of the valued services rendered to my Division by the company and of the soldierly spirit displayed at all times by	

Army Form C. 2118.

WAR DIARY
or
INTELLIGENCE SUMMARY.
(Erase heading not required.) C.R.E. 50TH DIVISION

Hour, Date, Place	Summary of Events and Information	Remarks and references to Appendices
19.6.15 GHQ SHEET 28	The officers, N.C.O.s. and men, and I congratulate the 50th Division on having at their disposal the services of this fine and efficient unit of the Territorial Force, whose departure we keenly regret, by me and by all ranks of the Division whilst in my Command. (sd) E.H. Bulfin, Major General Commanding 28th Division HEADQUARTERS 16th June 1915 C.R.E. The G.O.C. has very great pleasure in forwarding the above and congratulates the unit referred to in such high terms from Genl Bulfin. 18/6/15 (sd) Walter N. Lindsay Cmd 50th Div Maj Genl The above letter has been forwarded MAJOR PILLARD.	

18

Army Form C. 2118.

WAR DIARY
or
INTELLIGENCE SUMMARY.
(Erase heading not required.) C.R.E. 50TH DIVISION

Hour, Date, Place	Summary of Events and Information	Remarks and references to Appendices
19.6.15 G.D.L SHEET 28	Instructions received that the section of Chemical Experts R.E. at present attached to HQ 50th Div. R.E. will be discontinued & the department of this unit be transferred to the HQ 50 Div R.E. The transfer will take place on 21st inst. Extract from 50th Div. Operation Order No. 6 dated 18/6/15 — Para. 2. From 20th June Field Cos R.E. will be affiliated to Infantry Bdes. as follows:— Northumbrian Field Co. R.E. to 149th Inf Bde 2nd " " " " " " " 150th " 2nd N. Field Coy R.E. to 151st " The 2nd/2nd Co R.E. will proceed with 151st Inf Bde in the morning of 20th June from Elzen of Ouderdom. Road junction 83.0.y.15 to 9.6 amt north Zevecoten. Loc. Rg—Dranoutre by 6 a.m. next day. The 2nd/2nd Co N.D.R.E. will be given to the 149th Inf Bde on the morning of 21st from being clear of Ouderdom by 9.0 am. Route Zevecoten—Lo.Rg—Dranoutre via Meteren Clytte. The 2nd/2nd Andre will move with the 150th Inf Bde on the morning of 24th June being clear Ouderdom by 9 am + moving by Zevecoten to Lo.Rg.	

Army Form C. 2118.

WAR DIARY
or
INTELLIGENCE SUMMARY.
(Erase heading not required.) CRE 50TH DIVISION

Instructions regarding War Diaries and Intelligence Summaries are contained in F.S. Regs., Part II. and the Staff Manual respectively. Title pages will be prepared in manuscript.

Hour, Date, Place	Summary of Events and Information	Remarks and references to Appendices
19.6.15 G.27.b SHEET 28 11.46 am 20.6.15	Divisional HQ will move at 10 am 23rd June to M.31.b central. Then Wire No 1285 a/19/6/15 received from CE 5 Corps that Lieut SLADE + party will arrive HQ R.E. in morning probably in connection with the above.	
11.1 am do	Lieut Ino reviewed by me. 10.0 am Lieut SLADE CRE reported for Lieut ROBERTSON and CHEMICAL EXPERT 9 R.E. Left with ADJUTANT to see CRE 46th DIV with reference to number of Latrines in 2 the 528 DIV. Lieut GREEK AVC evacuated to hospital. Work carried on at HOOGE + north of	
2.30 pm do	3.0 pm Reported at M.J. 50 & DAS work carried out on line HOOGE - I.30.E.	
9.0 am 21.6.15 do	Proceeded with Adjutant to new area. Visited ST JANS CAPPEL with reference to billets for DHQ RE horses. At BAILEUL saw RE construction arranged for timber + stone dump. Saw O.C. 1st MONMOUTH RE with reference to him to be taken over by 149 Inf Bde + 2 NORTHUMBRIAN TO Co RE.	
10.30 am do do		

WAR DIARY
INTELLIGENCE SUMMARY
C.R.E. 50TH DIVISION

Army Form C. 2118.

Hour, Date, Place	Summary of Events and Information	Remarks and references to Appendices
21.6.15 Q27d. SHEET 28	Saw O.C. 2nd MONMOUTH RE with reference to his to be taken over by 151st Inf Bde & 7th Fd. Co. R.E. & also Major SYMONS R.E. O.C. of that unit, who had been over the line during the day with the O.C. 2/1st Co. M. R.E. Saw Sergt. J.E. POLLARD D.S.O. & Cpl. J. INSER, & accompany O.C. 1/2 N.R.E. & advised him further of his return. Extract from first Div 33 Appointments. Commun- Reward: D/n 16/15 2/7q. "The following men have been awarded the Distinguished Conduct Medal for acts of gallantry & devotion to duty in the field." Sergt. POLLARD No 1126 & Cpl. D.J. BROWN 31 NORTHUMBRIAN No 1138 & Sapper W.M. FAIRLESS Field Co. R.E. (T.F.) 2nd Lieut ROBERTSON with Lieut SLADE & Chemical Expert Section proceeded to 5th Corps where they are	
10.30 am	" " attached to 2nd Bde. Capt J.A. McQUEEN R.E. proceeded T. ZILLEBEKE Village with Major ACKERMAN S.O. V Corps and Major HOWARD R.E. O.C. 7th Fd Co R.E. & explained	

WAR DIARY
INTELLIGENCE SUMMARY.
(Erase heading not required.) CRE 50TH DIVISION

Army Form C. 2118.

21

Hour, Date, Place	Summary of Events and Information	Remarks and references to Appendices
22.6.15 A27h SHEET 28	nature of work being carried out there. 2 Lieut EASE, NDRE accompanied Major COWANS O.C. 175TH Co R.E. to front line trenches with reference to mining.	
7.0 p.m. do. do.	The following alterations are made to O.R. No 8 of 19/6/15. DIVL H.Q. will arrive at 10.0 am 24/6/15 T.M. 31.b central. 150TH Infy Bde will be relieved by 134TH Infy Bde on night of 23/24 June. The change of command will take place at 1-noon on that day. 150TH Infy Bde & 2nd NORTH FIELD & R.E. & No.4 DIVL TRAIN will march to 25TH June.	
7.45 am 23.6.15 do	C.S.O. Col HORDERN telephoned that Capt E.C. BURNUP O.C. 2nd Col C. N.D.R.E. had to meet the G.S.O.2 Major BONHAM CARTER at VLAMERTINGHE to go over the front line trenches. He also wished the C.R.E. & adjt. to go over the G.H.Q. line - ZILLEBEKE in the afternoon.	
12.30 p.m. do do.	Capt JA McQUEEN R.E. adjt proceeded to BAILLEUL, No1 fro 149 st - 151st Infy Bde - 7TH DR R.E. + 1st Fd G NDRE	

22

Army Form C. 2118.

WAR DIARY
or
INTELLIGENCE SUMMARY.
(Erase heading not required.) C.R.E. 50TH DIVISION.

Hour, Date, Place	Summary of Events and Information	Remarks and references to Appendices
23.6.15 6.27.b SHEET 28	with reference to taking over our line 23rd. WKK carried on drying right on defences. ZILLEBEKE by 2nd & 3rd N.F.R.E. (No Infantry working party available) for	
9.30am 24.6.15 6.27.b SHEET 28	Marched via WESTOUTRE & ST. JANS CAPPEL. Billetted Priest House. Room of mess offices. Two bedrooms. Accompanied by Adjutant went to BILLEUL R.E. trenches Stores. Fiesta offering to supply & works. Brigades for Received message from Col. HORDERN G.S.O.1 Stanham Div at 9.0am to Hd Qrs II Corps BAILLEUL. Saw Brig. Gen. + Chief Engineer Brig. Gen. HEATH. Went with them one part of the new other now by the 50TH DIV. to relieve.	
6.30 pm 25.6.15 St. JANS CAPPEL	Agnes of KEMMEL Accompanied by Adjutant Capt Jr MCQUEEN R.E. met MAJOR G.B.B. SYMONDS R.E. O.C.7TH FD.CO. R.E. at LINDENHOEK & inspected the new line he is working on with the 151ST INF. BDE. 3.0 pm	

(73989) W.4141—463. 400,000. 9/14. H.&J.Ltd. Forms/C. 2118/10.

23

Army Form C. 2118.

WAR DIARY
or
INTELLIGENCE SUMMARY.
(Erase heading not required.)

C.R.E. 50TH DIVISION

Hour, Date, Place	Summary of Events and Information	Remarks and references to Appendices
3.0 pm 26.6.15 ST JANS CAPPEL.	Attended conference at Head Quarters with C.R.A. and Brigadier of 149th & 150th 151st Bdes. 9am	
8.0 am 27.6.15 do	Proceeded with ADJUTANT to inspect lines of trenches held by 149th Inf Bde, and Mess to Major G.C. POLLARD O.C. 1st 2nd C.R.D.R.E. Attended conference at HdQrs at 8.30 pm. Lieut Green reported for duty from tropical for neglect.	
8.30 am 28.6.15 do	Accompanied G.S.O.1 & ADJUTANT reconnoitred line from SOUTH MIDLAND FARM on WULVERGHEM— MESSINES at points 6.0 7.7 and line of FARMS named BURNT, ELBOW, COOKER POND, FRENCHMANS, POM POM — SPY — N 28 c, b, d with reference to advices at three points. The ADJUTANT Captn J. A. McQUEEN R.E. left at LINDENHOEK Zijn. MAJOR SYMONDS R.E. O.C. 7th 2nd Co. R.E. Engineer BHQ lines & KEMMEL defences. attended conference at HdQrs at 6.30 pm Pm	

WAR DIARY / INTELLIGENCE SUMMARY

(Erase heading not required.) C.R.E. 50TH DIVISION

Army Form C. 2118.

Hour, Date, Place	Summary of Events and Information	Remarks and references to Appendices
2.0 p.m. 29.6.15 ST JANS CAPPEL	Proceeded with ADJUTANT to BAILLEUL with reference to timber yard & trench supplies afterwards meeting to 1/2nd & 7th Cos R.E. to arrange for O.C.'s meeting tomorrow in line to find what is required. Attended conference at Divl H.Qrs Division at 6.30 p.m. with Capt. J.A. McQUEEN R.E. left to join a line of strong points between WULVERGHEM - LINDENHOEK with O.C.'s 1st & 2nd Field Cos. N.D.R.E. who are responsible in seeing the work carried through.	
8.30 a.m. 30.6.15 do.	Proceeded to BAILLEUR with reference to stores at R.E. Timber yard and then attended conference at 50th Divl. H.Qrs. at 6.30 p.m. Received instructions that second line of French (reserve) with dugouts is made in rear of & close to trenches in left sub sector that USPY FARM is put in state of defence &c.	
11.0 a.m. do.		

50th Division

Confidential

121/6357

War Diary
of
50th (North'n) Divisional
R.E.
from 1st July to 31st July
1915
(Volume III).

Army Form C. 2118.

WAR DIARY
or
INTELLIGENCE SUMMARY.
(Erase heading not required.)

Instructions regarding War Diaries and Intelligence Summaries are contained in F. S. Regs., Part II. and the Staff Manual respectively. Title pages will be prepared in manuscript.

Hour, Date, Place	Summary of Events and Information	Remarks and references to Appendices
	Diary of C.R.E. 50th Division for July 1915. A. Twigg Lt. Col. C.R.E. 50th Divn 1/7/15	

WAR DIARY
INTELLIGENCE SUMMARY.
(Erase heading not required.)

C.R.E. 50TH DIVISION.

Army Form C. 2118.

25.

Hour, Date, Place	Summary of Events and Information	Remarks and references to Appendices
1.7.15 ST JANS CAPPEL	Copy ans reviewed and handed to Lieut Reid. TRENCH HOWITZER SCHOOL BERTHEN and Mr CRE standing orders for the 50th Div from No 1 to No 23 Given to His administration. Capn & Adjt. See WD 29/6/15. No 4 KITE BALLOON section attached for instruction to 50 Div. See WD 27/7/15. Al go to two	
2.7.15 do	Proceeded with ADJUTANT to LINDENHOEK + see— Inspected SPY and POM POM FARMS + arranged joined 6 Group SYMONDS DSO O.C. 3rd ARC defences. Carried out lines + support trenches inspected work being carried out there. Also inspected GHQ line where CYCLISTS are opening out were the trench between LINDENHOEK + N 33d SHEET 28 SW. Went round wells + water supply for DRANOUTRE, LOCRE + district with St CAZE and rode to N.B.R.E. who has the matter in hand. Attended conference at SD Div HQ 6.30pm from	
3.7.15 do	Called at BAILLEUL on C.E. II CORPS with reference to plan of defence of KEMMEL. he said there was no one killed there but that it was going to be called on at a conference of Divisional commander tonight. It will probably be taken from the 5D Div. + handed over to the Cavalry. Also went into water supply	

26

Army Form C. 2118.

WAR DIARY
or
INTELLIGENCE SUMMARY.
(Erase heading not required.) C.R.E. 50TH DIVISION.

Instructions regarding War Diaries and Intelligence Summaries are contained in F.S. Regs., Part II. and the Staff Manual respectively. Title pages will be prepared in manuscript.

Hour, Date, Place	Summary of Events and Information	Remarks and references to Appendices
3.7.15 ST JANS CAPPEL	of LOCRE, DRANOUTRE & ST JANS CAPPEL with him.	
6.30 p.m. 4.7.15 do	Attended conference at 50th Div. Hd Qrs at 6.30 p.m. Arranged & had agreement signed with parties of Brewer at ST JANS CAPPEL for supply of water from his well for use of troops & inhabitants of KEMMEL called on.	
8.15 a.m. 5.7.15 do	Left our H.Q. for KEMMEL & BAILLEUL with Officer to O.C. 1st Corps R.E. & sent round G.H.Q. land & defence works in hand. Attended conference at Div. KEMMEL. Hd Qr at 5.30 p.m. Returned to Hd Qrs at Lord DUNDREW's m. Tent? 2nd Lieut. ____ 50th Division ____ join 50th Div. here	
10.0 a.m. 6.7.15 do	Joined C.E. II Corps at 50th Div. Hd Qrs & proceeded with him to DRANOUTRE & see O.C. 2nd LONDRE. There he inspected the three lines of that unit. 4th , 1st Co. R.E. Then proceeded to KEMMEL see O.C., 3rd Co. R.E. inspecting lines of trench.	

(73989) W.4141—463. 400,000. 9/14. H.&J. Ltd. Forms/C. 2118/10.

Army Form C. 2118.

WAR DIARY
INTELLIGENCE SUMMARY.
(Erase heading not required.)

C.R.E. 50TH DIVISION

22.

Hour, Date, Place	Summary of Events and Information	Remarks and references to Appendices
6.7.15 ST JANS CAPPEL	A strong party in war. Lieut B. Dudley arrived from England for duty with 1st & 2nd C. N.D.R.E. and 2nd Lt D.R. FORSTER for 2nd & C. N.D.R.E.	
3.30 pm do do	MAJOR J.W. DOUGLAS O.C. 2/1st 2nd C. N.D.R.E. reported arrival at ST JANS CAPPEL. Strength 6 officers 212 O.R. + 1 Interpreter. They are quartered in square S.1.&.8.& SHEET 28 I.S.W. km. The 2/1 2nd C. N.D.R.E. were inspected by the G.O.C. 50th Div in a field S.1.&.6.E. firm.	
10.0 am 7/7/15 do	Wire received from II Corps through 50th Div. H.Q. that 2/1 Field C. N.D.R.E. to this unit detailed to 28th Div. Detail for move to be made direct between Divisions concerned.	
7.0 am 8.7.15 do	In accordance with message received through 50th Div. H.Q. attended at H.Q. Engineers Office with C.R.E.s 5th + 28th Divs with reference to taking over material, transport & camps supervision of works on all trenches in front of H.Q.	
10.0 am do do		

28.

WAR DIARY
INTELLIGENCE SUMMARY.

CAPE 55TH DIVISION

Hour, Date, Place	Summary of Events and Information	Remarks and references to Appendices
10.0 a.m. 6/7/15 ST JANS CAPPEL	2nd line relieve (a) what can be provided from the Division & (b) what help is required from II Corps. Reported that our motor lorry was now required & that it was being applied for through the Division. Informed that 6 offs & 5 ORs would be taken to the CE Atelier, that all in front of that line own made the Division, two officers to be detailed on from 2nd Field RE Co on from 1st Field RE Co for supervision of work made CE on Staff Line. Casualty: Lieut B Duckly, 1st Flanders wounded in action. Message received from CPE 28th Div? that one officer & 28 Co 2nd RE should report to Major Kelsall RE at 9.30 a.m. & at H 32 L 37 P. A further message was received that one officer, 8/21 2nd Co NDRE should report at 9.0 and 1st N.D. Co North Midland RE at 10.0 & take over Ren	

Army Form C. 2118.

29

WAR DIARY
or
INTELLIGENCE SUMMARY.
(Erase heading not required.) CRE 5TH DIVISION

Hour, Date, Place	Summary of Events and Information	Remarks and references to Appendices
8.0 am 9.7.15 ST JANS CAPPEL	Officers detailed by Major Douglas O.C. 71st Co. N.D.R.E. Lieut TRIPPE subject to Major KELSALL & Lieut WALKER to O.C. 2/2nd R.E. LOC.R.E. Escort. Lieut L.H. DOUGLAS 2nd W.C.N.D.R.E. killed in action 9th.	
8.0 am 10.7.15 ds	Left with Capt McQUEEN R.E. ADJUTANT for inspection of front line & support trenches from WULVERGHEM to N36 6.1.6. 2/1st 7d C.N.D.R.E. left for LOCRE at 5.30 pm from 28th Division.	
7.30 am 11.7.15 d	Capt J.A. McQUEEN R.E. Adjutant proceeded to Trenches DIV 1ST 14 - E.I.R in square N 36 d with O.C. 2/2d C.N.D.R.E. & Bdr Major 15th left Bde for the purpose of deciding entering supports line from. Called on O.E. 2/5 Inf.B. with reference to taking over their fighting line working under Major KELSALL R.E. owing to drawn of rest in front line 1/2 7d C.N.D.R.E. CE stated this officer would be relieved from 13th inst.	
2.30 pm 12.7.15 ds	Called at Trenches Ypres & see men.	

30.

Army Form C. 2118.

WAR DIARY
INTELLIGENCE SUMMARY.
(Erase heading not required.) C.R.E. 50TH DIVISION

Hour, Date, Place	Summary of Events and Information	Remarks and references to Appendices
12.7.15 ST JANS CAPPEL	rail tramway which is to be tried between SOUVENIR FARM, WOLVERGHEM to RE FARM. gm	
13.7.15 do	Bodies received that the Division will move to front area. Called on C.E. II Corps with reference to move railway who decided to hand it over to the incoming Division. Called on O.Cs. 1st & 2nd Fd of N.D.R.E. with reference to work on tunnel line. gm	
10.30 a.m. 14.7.15 do	Left with adjutant to see C.R.E. 27th Div? with reference to taking over our line from them, went over work with him. Called at Nullet (?) 1 D 1st Fd. C. R.E. & saw Major SINGER R E afterwards going to sawmill l'ARMENTIERES which is run by 2) 1st Div? They are going to carry on there work although is the end of Nth so of Div? With exception of O.C. II Corps. gm	

WAR DIARY
INTELLIGENCE SUMMARY

Army Form C. 2118.

C.R.E. 50TH DIVISION

31.

Hour, Date, Place	Summary of Events and Information	Remarks and references to Appendices
14.7.15 ST JANS CAPPEL	Received 50th Divn Operation Order No. 11 dt 13/7/15. 5th Divn to move to the neighbourhood of ARMENTIÈRES & will be relieved in its present line as follows:— Night 14/15th July. (a) 1st Bde CANADIAN Divn will take over from right of 149th Infy Bde to trench C.4 inclusive. Command of this portion of front will pass to the G.O.C. CANADIAN Divn on completion of relief. (b) 150th Infy Bde will take over trenches D1 and D2 and S.P.5 – from 149th Infy Bde. Night 15/16th July. 84th Infy Bde & 28th Divn will take over the line at present held by 151st Infy Bde. Night 16/17th July. 85th Infy Bde of 28th Divn will take over trenches E6 inclusive to trench D1 inclusive from 150th Infy Bde. Command of this portion of front relieved to 28th Divn will pass to G.O.C. 28th Divn on completion of each relief. Details of relief will be arranged between Infy Bdes concerned.	

Army Form C. 2118.

WAR DIARY
or
INTELLIGENCE SUMMARY.
(Erase heading not required.) CRE 50TH DIVISION

Hour, Date, Place	Summary of Events and Information	Remarks and references to Appendices
14.7.15 ST JANS. CAPPEL	Completion of reliefs to be reported to Div HR. All rabble & trench stores will be left in position - taken over by relieving unit. 3. Orders for the move of the Div to a new area will be issued later. Div.	
15.7.15 do.	ANNEX *SO has been appointed CRE 50TH DIVN. 50TH DIV Operation order No.12 d/15/7/15 reference [illegible] to aln No11. 1. The Division will assemble in area as shown in attached march table. [illegible] move of 150 the front takes [illegible] Infantry on night 16/15. 149th Infy Byp on night 17th from the night of 18/15, 151st Infy Bde will take over the right of Trench. 6) [illegible] ARMENTIERES. WE 2 MACQUART signed by Capt G. Trench [illegible] from 21 and 50 Div. Infy. to 15 Div. [illegible]	

WAR DIARY
INTELLIGENCE SUMMARY.
C.R.E. 50TH DIVISION.

Army Form C. 2118.

33.

Hour, Date, Place	Summary of Events and Information	Remarks and references to Appendices
15.7.15 ST JANS CAPPEL	Remain affiliated to the 151st Infy Bde. 3. At midnight 17/18th G.O.C. 50th Divn will resume command of our front. 5th Divl H.Q. will remain in present position until further orders. The 150th Inf Bde + 2nd Fd Co NDRE will move on the night of 17th + will be billeted about PONT DE NIEPPE. The 7th Fd C.R.E. + 1st Fd C. NDRE will billet in the HOSPICE DES ALIGNES, ARMENTIERES. 8 i 2 a central SHEET 36. km.	
16.7.15 ST JANS CAPPEL	Proceeded with Adjutant to ARMENTIERES with reference to workshop + dump for R.E. Stores called at billets (11) th Fd C. R.E. + saw Lt Col SINGER D.S.O. R.E. who takes over tonight as C.R.E. 50TH DIVISION. Rm.	

34.

Army Form C. 2118.

WAR DIARY
INTELLIGENCE SUMMARY.
(Erase heading not required.)

C.R.E. 50TH DIVISION

Instructions regarding War Diaries and Intelligence Summaries are contained in F. S. Regs., Part II. and the Staff Manual respectively. Title pages will be prepared in manuscript.

Hour, Date, Place	Summary of Events and Information	Remarks and references to Appendices
17.7.15. JAN. CAPPEL	Lt Col C.W. Singer D.S.O. returned to ARMENTIERES from sick leave & of 51 Divn H'Qrs in that town. F.E. H.Q. & F.E. Park R.E. Co. arrived & taken respective billets last night.	
18.7.15 JAN CAPPEL	2nd Field Co. R.E. marched to billets near PONT DE NIEPPE tonight. [town?] B.19.c.	
	19th [Fd?] Bdge. with my Brigadier from flight of Bruce W. on ARMENTIERES - WEZ MACQUART Road & left of Trenches (S.5. W.) from there to H.Q. Brigr.	
	4th D. Co R.E. in attack of Rue Bdge.	
	1st & 2nd Bdges RA in Trenches on night 18/7/15 from right trenches H.(5.a.y) to left of Trenches [Co.3.y?.30] found by 1st Bdge	
	1st Bde A.G. M.G. in [redoubt?] & Rue Bdge.	
	Reports [fo?] from the Park in RONDE WARP, ARMENTIERES.	
	Went to C.R.E. 17 Divn who [offered?] to supply of works.	
	+ G. let us known from billy & new POTINE SINGHS to complete defensive line & DUNKIRK. 25 Posts by C.W. are all [to extend?]	

(73989) W4141—463. 400,000. 9/14. H.&J.Ltd. Forms/C. 2118/10.

Army Form C. 2118.

WAR DIARY
or
INTELLIGENCE SUMMARY.
(Erase heading not required.)

Instructions regarding War Diaries and Intelligence Summaries are contained in F. S. Regs., Part II. and the Staff Manual respectively. Title pages will be prepared in manuscript.

Hour, Date, Place	Summary of Events and Information	Remarks and references to Appendices
19/7/15 ST. JAN CAPPEL	T.C. R.E.s took over the work with 152nd Inf. Bgde. & ready to install in I. 2 a. HOSPICE DES ALIGNES. Visited by S.C. 157th Inf. Bgde.	
20/7/15 ST. JAN-CAPPEL	Into ARMENTIERES to read to Capt. & arrange for work in right of Stores. Started a Div. W.L. Yard in RUE DES Attended conference at D.H.Q. at 6.30 p.m. as usual.	
21/7/15 ARMENTIERES	Div. H.Q. also moved into ARMENTIERES Today. to 24 RUE DE SARDIS - CARNOT. Capt. Brit Queens went on leave to England. Visited both Fd Coys. from Div. G.O.C. as usual.	
22/7/15 ARMENTIERES	Inspected Subordinary Lines. Interviewed Major Holdroyd R.E. O.C 42' G. Cos., who stated he was coming to took as Saturday Lines. Interviewed O.C 17th Tunnelling Cos. R.E. & C. Rec. 12 Div. Saw G. O.C. as usual.	

Army Form C. 2118.

WAR DIARY
or
INTELLIGENCE SUMMARY.
(Erase heading not required.)

Instructions regarding War Diaries and Intelligence Summaries are contained in F. S. Regs., Part II. and the Staff Manual respectively. Title pages will be prepared in manuscript.

Hour, Date, Place	Summary of Events and Information	Remarks and references to Appendices
23/7/15 ARMENTIERES	Inspected outer line of defended localities in area of outstanding line. Inspected by M.O. 15 Line & La Vesée trenches. Saw Div. G.O.C. at usual hour.	2nd Lt Votts & arrived from 2 Lt Cave & attached to 15 Brde. Fd Cy R.E.
24/7/15 ARMENTIERES	Inspected LA VESÉE and GROS POT trenches & reported to C.E. 2nd Corps on defensive lines. Arranged to meet D.C. 42nd Div. this afternoon at 2.30 p.m. to decide on work in Intending Line. Saw Div. G.O.C. at usual hour.	
25/7/15 ARMENTIERES	Visited 2nd Trenches & inspected except M.G. Cupolas & two turnouts in morning. Saw D.C.R. for firm to Capture & Inspection Mounts. Returned to town by 1 p.m. ago. Saw Div. G.O.C. at usual hour.	
26/7/15 ARMENTIERES	Visited front trenches with O.C. 1st Suffolk 15 Co. R.E. & inspected M.G. Cupolas. answers attend and on Support Trenches on left. Consulted G.O.C. 15 Bde 2nd Corps. Drove Drill for trench & Dugfs. Hand went R.E.G.C. Dein. All referred & heard P.G. & Hand Grenades by Capt Genchen, 2 Corps.	

Army Form C. 2118.

WAR DIARY
or
INTELLIGENCE SUMMARY.
(Erase heading not required.)

Instructions regarding War Diaries and Intelligence Summaries are contained in F.S. Regs., Part II. and the Staff Manual respectively. Title pages will be prepared in manuscript.

Hour, Date, Place	Summary of Events and Information	Remarks and references to Appendices
27/7/15 ARMENTIERES.	Visited Front & Intry diary lines with Brig- Genl. Heath, C.E. 2" Corps in morning. Visited Hd. Qrs - F.A. Corps in afternoon. Usual interviews with Div. g.o.c.	Lieut. E.D. CASE, 2nd Northumberland Fus. L.M.G. officer.
28/7/15 ARMENTIERES.	Visited Front & Subsidiary lines with Capt. Int. Queen in morning. Attended funeral of Lt. Cave & inspected Hd. Qrs. Usual interviews with Div. G.O.C. - settled various private cases. Subsidiary line.	
29/7/15 ARMENTIERES.	Visited Front & Supports lines & inspected Farm Concrete M.G. Emplacements Visited G.O.C. 151st Bde. & arranged for Brigade Musing Fusn. to be attached to 2nd Batt. R.G.R. Usual visit with Div. G.O.C.	

(73989) W4141—463. 400,000. 9/14. H.&J.Ltd. Forms/C. 2118/10.

Army Form C. 2118.

WAR DIARY
or
INTELLIGENCE SUMMARY.
(Erase heading not required.)

Instructions regarding War Diaries and Intelligence Summaries are contained in F.S. Regs., Part II. and the Staff Manual respectively. Title pages will be prepared in manuscript.

Hour, Date, Place	Summary of Events and Information	Remarks and references to Appendices
ARMENTIERES 29/7/15	Took luncheon [?] with Ferro-Concrete Emplacements in Vicinity. Line & made various experiments. Canadian Division M.G. Officer accompanied me. Visited 171st Tunnelling Co. HQ in afternoon. Attended meeting at Divl Office ad 4 pm re use of Rn.G. 2nd Corps, subject "Water Supply". Met Corps Commander, Sir Charles Ferguson at Div. of 2nd Corps.	
ARMENTIERES 30/7/15	Inspected firing line of 8 M.G. with suggestions re improved bracket & improved mounting, notes on June 844.	

C. A. Sugar [?] Lt. Col. M
C. M. G. 5th Div.

121/6550

50th Division

H’d q’rs R.E. 50th Division

Vol IV

From 1st to 31st Aug. 1915

Army Form C. 2118.

WAR DIARY
or
INTELLIGENCE SUMMARY.

(Erase heading not required.)

C.RE. 50th Divn.

From 1st August 1915
To 31st August 1915

[signature]
C.RE. 50th Divn.

31/8/15

Army Form C. 2118.

WAR DIARY
or
INTELLIGENCE SUMMARY.
(Erase heading not required.)

Instructions regarding War Diaries and Intelligence Summaries are contained in F.S. Regs., Part II. and the Staff Manual respectively. Title pages will be prepared in manuscript.

Hour, Date, Place	Summary of Events and Information	Remarks and references to Appendices
ARMENTIERES. 1/8/15	Inspected Front & Support Line, also portion of Subsidiary Line. Reconnoitred positions for bridges over River Lys. Usual visit to F.O.C. Div. Capt [?] Queens took of Hill 63 & our Snipers in afternoon. Reported had eight rounds of Trench in Enemy Trench 74 [?] & seven sleep in't. (Wounded & dying getting removed to Trench 61 in River to be evacuated).	
ARMENTIERES 2/8/15	Inspected Front & Support Line & also middle portion of Subsidiary Line. Laws has new 13-42 Oro Eng-Brig-Bdr & gave details supplying them, also new Turs - Guests M.G. Supplements in Trench 75. Visited new F.C. Companies & H.G. Party in aft. Regiment Home to BAILLEUL Day various bits. Usual visit to Div H.O.C.	

Army Form C. 2118.

WAR DIARY
or
INTELLIGENCE SUMMARY.

(Erase heading not required.)

Instructions regarding War Diaries and Intelligence Summaries are contained in F.S. Regs., Part II. and the Staff Manual respectively. Title pages will be prepared in manuscript.

Hour, Date, Place	Summary of Events and Information	Remarks and references to Appendices
ARMENTIERES 3/9/15	Visited Right Brigade Front & Support Trenches, also Artillery. Lar in morning. Capt Smith from C.E. 2nd Corps came to see me with reference to moving light railways — explained my views to him. Visited M.G. Emplacement close to PONT-DE-NIEPPE, also 27th Div. M.G. Park in afternoon. Kienast went to Div. G.O.C.	
ARMENTIERES 4/9/15	Conferences; settled on him head of Artillery Lord with Div G.O.C. in morning. Visited the Corps in afternoon, then attended a meeting at Div H.Q. in question. [?] prepared of notes for Corps & Commanders for this Command put up as heading par 22 Div G Corps formed Settlement	
ARMENTIERES 5/9/15	Inspected Front & Subsidiary lines with Capt Pitt. Breen in morning. Wrote to Corps & H.Q. Pack in afternoon. Round about & in by 17.25	Yesterday etc. as to RE. [?]

Army Form C. 2118.

WAR DIARY
or
INTELLIGENCE SUMMARY.
(Erase heading not required.)

Instructions regarding War Diaries and Intelligence Summaries are contained in F.S. Regs., Part II. and the Staff Manual respectively. Title pages will be prepared in manuscript.

Hour, Date, Place	Summary of Events and Information	Remarks and references to Appendices
ARMENTIERES 6/8/15	Inspected Front Lines of Right Brigade & Subsidiary Line in morning. Major Sankey, D.I.O. R.E. O.C. 1st Field Squadron R.E. called with reference to work in hand on outskirts of ARMENTIERES. Visited C.R.E. 27th Div. in afternoon. Usual visit to Div. G.O.C.	
ARMENTIERES 7/8/15	Visited Front Line & inspected Concrete M.G. Emplac in Trenches 69 & 74 - also clear Support Trenches & Subsidiary Line on south. Inspected M.G. Emplac in HOUPLINES Cemetery & 8 month in afternoon. Capt Smith R.E., R.E. Engineer 2nd Corps called & arranged for meeting on 9th with re selection & works of Trenches to Front Trenches. Usual visit to Div. G.O.C.	
ARMENTIERES 8/8/15	Inspected Subsidiary Line in morning & selected M.G. Emplacements. Lt. Col. Williams R.E. C.R.E. 12th Div. to Trenches 78 & 74 & tour arrangements. J. Emplt accounts in afternoon. Visited this Coy & arranged about Stones, Sandbags & nots of crucial drag-outs. Capt Sinor 2nd F.D. Squadron R.E. came tree me the orders.	
ARMENTIERES 9/8/15	Inspected R.H. Bdge Front Trenches & Subsidiary Line, selected position for M.G. & Trench. Arranged for Classes of Instruction in M.G. for bodge in trenches. 1 Batt of 37th Div. moved in for work in Subsidiary Line.	

(73989) W4141—463. 400,000. 9/14. H.&J.Ltd. Forms/C. 2118/10.

Army Form C. 2118.

WAR DIARY
or
INTELLIGENCE SUMMARY.
(Erase heading not required.)

Instructions regarding War Diaries and Intelligence Summaries are contained in F.S. Regs., Part II and the Staff Manual respectively. Title pages will be prepared in manuscript.

Hour, Date, Place	Summary of Events and Information	Remarks and references to Appendices
ARMENTIERES 10/8/15	Visited Left Bdge. area in front & behind firing line in morning. Noticed various points as to construction of machine gun emplacements. Infty. Bn. Fd. Companies & RE. Task in afternoon. Went round to G.O.C. Division. C.R.E. also suggested use of a "sniper loophole" i.e. a small plate of workshops. Trench boardwalks.	
ARMENTIERES 11/8/15	Inspected Right Bdge. area in front, support & subsidiary lines in morning. Gave orders as to method of construction of MG. post in centre line. Saw Div. G.O.C. at 2.30 p.m. re Training of troops & various matters of secrecy. noise underground. Visited a.C.E. at 3.30 p.m. inspected pill boxes about subsidiary line.	
ARMENTIERES 12/8/15	Visited Rt. Bdge. front trenches & subsidiary lines in morning. Inspected foot bridges which subsidiary line. in afternoon. Inspected site at PONT DE NIEPPE and bridge in C/S. & Rt. prepared for demoln. Went round R.E. & C. Bn.	
ARMENTIERES 13/8/15	Inspected Left Bdge. front Trenches & Subsidiary Line in morning. Visited Field Companies & RE. Task in afternoon. Gave orders for designs & to prepare for new Travel Bridge over River L.S.	

(73989) W4141—463. 400,000. 9/14. H.&J.Ltd. Forms/C. 2118/10.

Army Form C. 2118.

42

WAR DIARY
or
INTELLIGENCE SUMMARY.
(Erase heading not required.)

Instructions regarding War Diaries and Intelligence Summaries are contained in F.S. Regs., Part II. and the Staff Manual respectively. Title pages will be prepared in manuscript.

Hour, Date, Place	Summary of Events and Information	Remarks and references to Appendices
ARMENTIERES. 14/8/15	Inspected Left Bdge. Front & Support Trenches with Brigadier in morning. Visited by O.C. 153rd Bde. in afternoon about subject of Misc. Engineering Claims, also 17 Co. who re drew old H.Q. V.2.L.N.03 in new drawing.	
ARMENTIERES 15/8/15	Lots of German mining in Jor Trench — as result Allowed Church Parade where G.O.C. Div. presents D.C.M. to 2nd Corpl Brown. Attended 2nd Lt. Case's funeral in afternoon. Men visited cleared at HOUPLINES.	2nd Lieut. P.E. CASE — Killed on night of 8/14/15. No. 1276. 2nd Corporal O.I. BROWN, 15 him 2. Co. M. presented with D.C.M.
ARMENTIERES 16/8/15	Inspected Rd. Bryan Front Trenches & Subsidiary Line in morning. New Fire-Trench M.G. Emplacs. commenced in Trench 71 to cover front of "Mushroom". Inspected Loft of Subsidiary Line in afternoon. Put up an experimental M.G. Emplac. Genl. Nail to G.O.C. Div.	
ARMENTIERES 17/8/15	Inspected new Bdge. Dug-out at HOUPLINES — arranged about Trenching this work — new M.G. Emplac. M.G. Emplaces. in 80 & 91. Visited Div. H.Q. Geo. & A loys. in afternoon — saw 62 & 2 Co. Genl. Nail to Div. G.O.C.	

Army Form C. 2118.

44

WAR DIARY
or
INTELLIGENCE SUMMARY.

(Erase heading not required.)

Instructions regarding War Diaries and Intelligence Summaries are contained in F.S. Regs., Part II. and the Staff Manual respectively. Title pages will be prepared in manuscript.

Hour, Date, Place	Summary of Events and Information	Remarks and references to Appendices
ARMENTIERES. 18/8/15	Inspected subsidiary line & drainage in morning, also internal enfilements. Scheme of trenches on Chapelle D'Armentières Rd. Visited 17th Divn area in afternoon & saw subsidiary line. Hand over to G.O.C. Divn.	
ARMENTIERES 19/8/15	Visited Front line & inspected Concrete M.G. Emplacements — also subsidiary lines in morning. Visited Bde Commanders Rt Sect in afternoon.	
ARMENTIERES 20/8/15	G.O.C. Divn inspects subsidiary line this morning. Walked to coy in afternoon.	
ARMENTIERES 21/8/15	Inspected Rd. Bdge. Front & Support Trenches in morning — also subsidiary line & concrete M.G. Emplacements. Inspects New targets on River Lys in afternoon continuing bridging material. Hand visit to Div. G.O.C.	

Army Form C. 2118.

45

WAR DIARY
or
INTELLIGENCE SUMMARY.
(Erase heading not required.)

Instructions regarding War Diaries and Intelligence Summaries are contained in F.S. Regs., Part II. and the Staff Manual respectively. Title pages will be prepared in manuscript.

Hour, Date, Place	Summary of Events and Information	Remarks and references to Appendices
ARMENTIERES 22/8/15	Inspected Left Bde. Front & Support Trenches & new earwork. Machine Guns Coyl assembled, also drainage & new Bdge. H.Qrs. Inspected Left Subsidiary Line. Visits 42nd Co. & 20th Field Coys. in afternoon. Usual visit to Divl. G.O.C.	
ARMENTIERES 23/8/15	Inspected HOU PLINES Railway Bridge as Cavalry wanted to and a barge to make another bridge. Later visited Half Mile wood to ascertain. Visited N.E. Post 2&2 CoHQ Workshops, also "Wells" "Barges in afternoon. Usual visit to G.O.C. Div. Capt. Hickman 14th 171st Tunneling Co. to divisional hours.	
ARMENTIERES 24/8/15	Inspected Right Bdge. Front Trenches & went into question of drainage of Communication Trenches. 42nd Co. 8th capturing and digging sap, where moved to A.P.D. Went to Bdge. in afternoon. Inspected gun revetments. Saw men at work & arranging to move of Communication Trenches in parties. Usual visit to Divl. G.O.C.	

Army Form C. 2118.

WAR DIARY
or
INTELLIGENCE SUMMARY.
(Erase heading not required.)

Instructions regarding War Diaries and Intelligence Summaries are contained in F. S. Regs., Part II. and the Staff Manual respectively. Title pages will be prepared in manuscript.

Hour, Date, Place	Summary of Events and Information	Remarks and references to Appendices
ARMENTIERES 25/8/15	Inspected & chose positions for 2 Support Points with Div. G.S.O. in morning. Examined shells and RL 13" MH Gun. heavy and FMZE DE LA BUTERNE in position in afternoon. Inspected site for Machine Gun Emplacement in infantry line in fosses.	
ARMENTIERES 26/8/15	Found best site for support point 6 O.C. 12 Batt. 23 C.M.R. then inspected cementl H.G. Emplacements in Trenches 75, 76, 80, also Point in Trench 80. In afternoon visited 6.2 to 12 with Adjt. and Asst R.C. Secretary Later in battn at POINT DE NIEPPE O.C. 1/7/3 Fusiliers Capt. H. Cole as to putting action LILLE POST. Visited rail site for Support Point. H.D.C 2 back to Co.Hd. Sub inspected front line & PONT LUSINE Support Point and O.C. 2/2 Y&L at 5.30 pm returned with form Secretary, Gen. visited Hd. Corps. Went round to Div. G.O.C.	

Army Form C. 2118.

WAR DIARY
or
INTELLIGENCE SUMMARY.
(Erase heading not required.)

Instructions regarding War Diaries and Intelligence Summaries are contained in F. S. Regs., Part II. and the Staff Manual respectively. Title pages will be prepared in manuscript.

Hour, Date, Place	Summary of Events and Information	Remarks and references to Appendices
ARMENTIERES 28/8/15	Visited Hd. Qrs. in morning re: Security Report on Defences. Visited new Battery at ROMARIN in afternoon with Capt. Hd. Qrs. Usual visit to Div. J.O.C.	
	Legal Dept commenced report on N. side of LILLE ROAD behind Trench 67. Commencing on S. south side bridge. Inspected Fd. Bdge C. Trenches, Subsidiary Line also new Support Point. Saw Hd. Qrs. (21st Regt.) in Lt. B. Williams Report on position.	
ARMENTIERES 29/8/15	Inspected Cp. in aft. — usual visit via Div. J.O.C. Visited Caps in aft. — usual visit via Div. J.O.C. Inspected Dug-outs for Fd. Bdge. Portable Obs also new Off. Bdge. Obs & Interior Lines arrangement. Saw O.C. 2nd R.C. Re: arrangement of trenches opening in Tr. 70. Usual visit to Div. J.O.C.	
ARMENTIERES 31/8/15	Went to Hd. Qrs. re Germans crossing against Tr. 70. — Went to G.H.Q. 13th Div. for conference with C.E. 2nd Corps & other new types of work. Had lunch there & had tea there in afternoon. Usual visit to Div. J.O.C.	

J. Twyn Col M
C.R.E. 5th Div.

12/6930

50th Division

Hd Qrs R.E. 50th Division
Int
Sept 15

War Diary
of
C.R.E. 50th Division.
To
September 1915.

WAR DIARY
or
INTELLIGENCE SUMMARY.
(Erase heading not required.)

Army Form C. 2118.

Hour, Date, Place	Summary of Events and Information	Remarks and references to Appendices
ARMENTIERES 1/9/15	Inspected two new supporting points also (4) & (4), with Div. G.O.C. in morning, also subsidiary line. Gen. Sir H.S. Rawlinson in afternoon - touched for bridges. Gone in of all different ranges. General visit to Div. G.O.C.	
ARMENTIERES 2/9/15	Inspected Rd. Rouge, Front trenches in morning, including new light railway, and M.G. dugouts in Tr. 69 & drainage of 121TH M.A.R. Inspected Phillips aux. Rein. cov. & afternoon presently ready for demolition. General visit to Div. G.O.C.	
ARMENTIERES 3/9/15	Very wet - working parties on new supporting points also very busy with last night's Inspected front & subsidiary lines in morning. Horses on sewer in trenches 67 & 70 to 71, at Tunnelling C.T. General visit to Div. G.O.C.	

Army Form C. 2118.

49

WAR DIARY
or
INTELLIGENCE SUMMARY.
(Erase heading not required.)

Instructions regarding War Diaries and Intelligence Summaries are contained in F.S. Regs., Part II. and the Staff Manual respectively. Title pages will be prepared in manuscript.

Hour, Date, Place	Summary of Events and Information	Remarks and references to Appendices
ARMENTIERES 4/9/15	Major Pollard 1st N.Mx. M.G.W. returned from leave. Received notice that attack was expected at 9 a.m. on oxygen wind to Battn. Oro. – 9 & Div. Hd Qrs. – relieved from Mess at 12.30 p.m. Tour in Defensive Line made by Cavalry with H.Ch. Hopkins at 2.30 p.m. Conference of Brigadiers at Div. H.d Qrs. at 3 p.m. Supplies having in R.I. Regts. area a fresh Trenches in autumn very wet. Enemy out for 2 hours from Bridges North of PONT DE NIEPPE in afternoon. Usual visit to Div. G.O.C.	
ARMENTIERES 5/9/15		
AR MENTIERES 6/9/15	Reconnoitred ground between Lefford & subsidiary lines in morning with view of obtaining a correct approach in each ground in afternoon. Enemy shelling rather more persistent than usual. Usual visit to Div. G.O.C.	

Army Form C. 2118.

57

WAR DIARY
or
INTELLIGENCE SUMMARY.
(Erase heading not required.)

Instructions regarding War Diaries and Intelligence Summaries are contained in F. S. Regs., Part II. and the Staff Manual respectively. Title pages will be prepared in manuscript.

Place	Date	Hour	Summary of Events and Information	Remarks and references to Appendices
ARMENTIERES	7/9/15		Attended Conference of C.R.E.s and C.E. officer at BAILLEUL at 11 a.m. Gen. Gough (C.E. 2 Army) & Staff there. (R.E. 2 Corps) and Lieuts Left Banks Front Support & Trench. Lines in afternoon. Party of F.17. DE. BUTERNE came to see me with regard to plan of entanglement across Stream leaving the points. Went round to D.H.Q. of 6th – he decides to commence making Concrete M.G. Cupolas in support line infantry & Battn for M.G. Gunners in Front Line.	
ARMENTIERES	8/9/15		Inspected new Cavalry Line in rear end of town with Div. G.O.C. in morning. Inspected reports on Bailly Bleu near PONT. DE. NIEPPE in afternoon. Went round to G.O.C. Div.	
ARMENTIERES	9/9/15		Inspected new evening position of new Cavalry Line with Div. G.O.C. in morning. Visited trench corps in afternoon. Went round to Div. G.O.C.	

Army Form C. 2118
57

WAR DIARY
or
INTELLIGENCE SUMMARY.
(Erase heading not required.)

Instructions regarding War Diaries and Intelligence Summaries are contained in F. S. Regs., Part II. and the Staff Manual respectively. Title pages will be prepared in manuscript.

Place	Date	Hour	Summary of Events and Information	Remarks and references to Appendices
ARMENTIERES	10/9/15		Enemy's new Support Points with Div. G.O.C. in morning – Enemy working party working on subsidiary line just west of CHAPELLE D'ARMENTIERES Cemetery had 2 killed & 12 wounded by one shell. Prospects this afternoon & also and front defeat in subsidiary line with Capt. Mc Queen in afternoon. Usual visit to Div. G.O.C.	
ARMENTIERES	11/9/15		Prospects what length of front line is missing – Enemy shelling rather heavily. Two new supporting Points getting on well. Prospects Rd. Park & horse power under construction in afternoon. Usual visit to Div. G.O.C.	
ARMENTIERES	12/9/15		Went to MONT NOIR with Brig. G.O.C. to see experiments of shooting 18pr. H.E. shell against various types of reinforced concrete walls. Visits to Coys. in afternoon.	

Army Form C. 2118

WAR DIARY
or
INTELLIGENCE SUMMARY.
(Erase heading not required.)

Instructions regarding War Diaries and Intelligence Summaries are contained in F. S. Regs., Part II. and the Staff Manual respectively. Title pages will be prepared in manuscript.

Place	Date	Hour	Summary of Events and Information	Remarks and references to Appendices
ARMENTIERES	13/9/15		Inspected Rgt. Regs. Front & Support Lines — also Supporting Point at EGALE & Subsidiary Line in morning. Inspected various bridges in afternoon & called on C.R.E. 27th Div. at CROIX-DU-BAC.	
ARMENTIERES	14/9/15		Inspected Front Line & Support Trenches on left in morning & also new Communication Trench from FIVE LE TARDIN & PLANK AVENUE in morning. Visited new Essel[?] pier bridge with Major Pollar[d?] R.E. Called upon G.O.C. G.A.G.	
ARMENTIERES	15/9/15		Inspected firstead[?] new Div. 15 addle H.[?]. Qtrs & also new Communication Trench & Subsidiary Line in morning. Inspected new Essel[?] pier bridge & T.T. Park in afternoon.	

Army Form C. 2118

53

WAR DIARY
or
INTELLIGENCE SUMMARY.
(Erase heading not required.)

Instructions regarding War Diaries and Intelligence Summaries are contained in F. S. Regs., Part II. and the Staff Manual respectively. Title pages will be prepared in manuscript.

Place	Date	Hour	Summary of Events and Information	Remarks and references to Appendices
ARMENTIERES	16/9/15		Inspected 124 Fd. Amb. & his new supporting points in evening. Visits. Reconnoitring sites & new communication Trench from F.M.E. DES JARDIN to PLANK ROAD. Usual visit to G.O.C. Div.	
ARMENTIERES	17/9/15		Inspected Recommendations for Honours for (1) 2nd Battn. Y.PRES in Report & Diary, (2) General service & good conduct in France. Inspected new barrel pier bridge. 2 Lt. Angus promoted on leave.	
ARMENTIERES	18/9/15		70 R.E. by telegram Transmissions. Nothing unusual to be on defensive line) instructions Orders received re gaining higher tests. Ring to the holders to be completed by night 24/25 ocht. D. Feilding started this week.	

Army Form C. 2118

54

WAR DIARY
or
INTELLIGENCE SUMMARY.
(Erase heading not required.)

Instructions regarding War Diaries and Intelligence Summaries are contained in F. S. Regs., Part II. and the Staff Manual respectively. Title pages will be prepared in manuscript.

Place	Date	Hour	Summary of Events and Information	Remarks and references to Appendices
ARMENTIERES	1/9/15		A/Director visited bivouacs & horse lines with Major Grubb in the morning & after. More shelter ought to be required.	
ARMENTIERES	2/9/15		A/Director inspected 5 in to steam boat - (Recent 4 supplts 4 supplies slightly damaged with an eight day stay on lowest side of the slaver, placed about 10" in front of timbers, then secondly lighted by steam teller worked in pannier-slown from tow track & makes an efficient smoke screen w- gives favourable wind.)	
ARMENTIERES	2/9/15		A/Director attended meeting of CRE's at CE of the Army. - (Suggs. gb to be field supplies to 30th Div in N. Div RE increased), 50-60 to be prov. lines at Butler bridge from Belloy's yard to NIEPPE for trans. to train). A/Director visited FORET DE NIEPPE & overseer are laying up of trenches there, also ESTAIRES Shonken Lanetes for train bridge.	

2353 Wt. W.2514/1454 700,000 5/15 D. D. & L. A.D.S.S. Forms/C. 2118

WAR DIARY
or
INTELLIGENCE SUMMARY.
(Erase heading not required.)

Army Form C. 2118

Place	Date	Hour	Summary of Events and Information	Remarks and references to Appendices
ARMENTIERES	22/9/15		Bright broken formation of clouds reported for 4 K^t home helio (not actuon at 6/30) & travel. Inst. letter quickly from there sent for DUNKERQUE) — 16 trucks of Stokes arrived for division between 5&5 and 1st Divn	
ARMENTIERES	23/9/15		Instructions received when 3 howi^r brigs Completed in position & training of 24/25 R — also Krupp Mushroom Trench & found for demolition under action circumstances — OC 170 Bg started from Pry —	
ARMENTIERES	24/9/15		Issue of Divn late Operation Order No 13 — Improvements made to howi^r Lys & lofty with new fin twenty tree dimention in opportunity occurring — (Mosiken — Swampy Ground shafts) M. G. entrenchments machine gun 3 howi^r brigs Completed to "position" by 10 hrs. — 42" Pr. in change of battery up epaules —	

2353 Wt. W3544/1454 700,000 5/15 D. D. & L. A.D.S.S. Forms/C. 2118.

Army Form C. 2118

57

WAR DIARY
or
INTELLIGENCE SUMMARY.
(Erase heading not required.)

Instructions regarding War Diaries and Intelligence Summaries are contained in F. S. Regs., Part II. and the Staff Manual respectively. Title pages will be prepared in manuscript.

Place	Date	Hour	Summary of Events and Information	Remarks and references to Appendices
ARMENTIERES	25/9/15		Heavy bombardment of enemy's trenches in early morning – very little reply from trenches prior to Battle Bn. Visits of G.O.C. Div in morning – 149 & 150 Brigs. H.Qtrs in afternoon. Genl of Br. Hd.Qrs. M.C. R.E. & Cols contd in morning. Visit to Br. G.O.C. Lieut Col. Pogo returned from leave.	
ARMENTIERES	26/9/15		Inspected 3 new trestle pier bridges in morning & reconnoitred routes to them. Inspected 3rd Div. R.E. Park in afternoon & decided on type of hut to be made. Col. Williams CRE 12 Div. informed me that 70 D Co. R.E. was to come under my orders. O.C. 1st Batt. R.E. took over duties today in new sector, viz Trenches 81-87 inclusive. Usual visit to Br. G.S.C.	
ARMENTIERES	27/9/15		Inspected new bridge abutting Lent to River & US with G.O.C. 150 Brigr. in morning. Brigr Bateman O.C. 70 Bn. C.O. R.E. In afternoon reconnoitred Southern Defences of ARMENTIERES with O.C. 2 Corps & Brigr Kennel, O.C. 6.2 Co. A.T. No. 3 73 Co. 50. latter away & reported 12 Div. tonight. Usual visit to Br. G.S.C.	

WAR DIARY
or
INTELLIGENCE SUMMARY.

Army Form C. 2118.

57

Place	Date	Hour	Summary of Events and Information	Remarks and references to Appendices
ARMENTIERES	28/9/15		Left H.Q. BAILLEUL at 8 a.m. & Took over duties of O.C. 2 Corps from Brig. Gen. G. H. HEATH M.S. Reported by Phone to RORIRAN & our Brigade Released M.S. & Went to ARMENTIERES. In afternoon inspected Retrenching lines from PLOEGSTRET to PONT BALLOT with Bregd Released I.D. Corps under Bregd Symons D.S.O. M.P. (Section) reported 50 Dev Engy.	
ARMENTIERES	29/9/15		Into BAILLEUL at 8 a.m. — moved C. 1 & Corps of 8th Labour Bri. to repost to Bregd Released M.P. at 8 a.m. Tournon for work on G.H.Q. 2 Line. Visited 171 Tunnelling Co. M.P. when C.R.E. (Lt. Col. Dotto R.E.) 25 Dev at NIEPPE. At Divisione met O.C. 9 Labour Bn. called to my two M.O. were retained north. Visited all Mess to Corps in aft. Went Round to Dir. G.O.C.	
ARMENTIERES	30/9/15		Into NIEPPE hut Lt.Col. Dotto R.E. C.M.E. 28 Div. Went to BAILLEUL to C.E's Office. Inspected with O.C. R.E. 2 Lines at PONT-DE-NIEPPE. Inspected lock at HOOPLINES also Supporting Tombs at BLANK and PORTE-EGAL Returned in aft. & new R.E. Bridge Built H.Q. Then Went Round to Dir. G.O.C.	

2333 Wt. W2514/1454 730,000 5/15 D.D. & L. A.D.S.S. Forms/C. 2118.

121/7333

H.Qrs R.E. 50th Division

Vol VI

Oct. 15

SECRET

War Diary
of
C.R.E. 50th Division.

From 1/10/15 to 31/10/15.

C. L. Singh Lt. Col. RE
C.R.E. 50 Div.

Army Form C. 2118

WAR DIARY
or
INTELLIGENCE SUMMARY.
(Erase heading not required.)

Instructions regarding War Diaries and Intelligence
Summaries are contained in F. S. Regs., Part II.
and the Staff Manual respectively. Title pages
will be prepared in manuscript.

Place	Date	Hour	Summary of Events and Information	Remarks and references to Appendices
ARMENTIERES	1/9/15			

WAR DIARY
or
INTELLIGENCE SUMMARY.
(Erase heading not required.)

Army Form C. 2118

Place	Date	Hour	Summary of Events and Information	Remarks and references to Appendices
ARMENTIERES	4/10/15		Inspects Right Bridge Front & Support lines also Infantry line with O.C. 2 North. H. Co. RE. Settled details of drainage & communication Trenches — completion of Support line at PONT BALLOT DE NIEPPE etc. Attended Conference of Bde Engineers at Div H.Qrs. C.R.E. 2.5 Div Corps to come to 5 Flag tomorrow in ARMENTIERES.	
ARMENTIERES	5/10/15		Inspects Center Bridge Front & Support lines & Subsidiary line in morning. Inspected approaches to Bavel piers, Bridges in afternoon with Capt. McQueen, also Rt. Park. Usual visit to Div. G.O.C.	
ARMENTIERES	6/10/15		Inspects Infantry Bridges & also small Bridges leading to Hinges Railway, also Subsidiary line South of PONT BALLOT & thence South to CHAPELLE D'ARMENTIERES South field Coys in afternoon. Usual visit to Div. G.O.C.	

Army Form C. 2118

WAR DIARY
or
INTELLIGENCE SUMMARY.
(Erase heading not required.)

Instructions regarding War Diaries and Intelligence Summaries are contained in F. S. Regs., Part II. and the Staff Manual respectively. Title pages will be prepared in manuscript.

Place	Date	Hour	Summary of Events and Information	Remarks and references to Appendices
ARMENTIERES	7/9/15		To CHAPELLE D'ARMENTIERES with Lt Col. Harben, G.S.O.1, 6ᵗʰ Div. & selected site for new communication Trench East of Rue du Tonn. Also selected site to which to move Pontoon Bridge. In afternoon inspected various Water Services of H.Q.2 Sect. at PONT DE NIEPPE. Usual visit to G.O.C. Div.	
ARMENTIERES	8/9/15		Inspected left Subs. Front & Support Lines with 50ᵗʰ Queens in morning. Inspected M.T. Post in afternoon & new site for Pontoon Bridge across today. C.E. & C.R.E. called to day / H.C.M. & 1 Sec. infantry of 4ᵗʰ Division coming for next weeks. Usual visit to Div. G.O.C.	
ARMENTIERES	9/9/15		Inspected Centre Bays Front & Support Lines with Major Pollard, 2 Co. M. of 1ˢᵗ North. R.E.M. related with G. 1ˢᵗ G. Cuplees & new Communication Trench. Inspected Horse Lines near PONT DE NIEPPE.	

2353 Wt. W2514/1454 700,000 5/15 D. D. & L. A.D.S.S. Forms/C. 2118.

WAR DIARY
or
INTELLIGENCE SUMMARY.

(Erase heading not required.)

Army Form C. 21

Place	Date	Hour	Summary of Events and Information	Remarks and references to Appendices
ARMENTIERES	10/10/15		With O.C. 2nd North M.C. Bde, Capt. Gifford, to select site for new Communication Trench from Rd. Bdge. Battn. H^d Qrs. to Town — also inspected firing position in PORTE EGAL C.T. Round Defences of Town in afternoon with Capt. Ge^o Queen, Brit C.RL. 25th Div.; arranged to have one of his R.E. Officers with each Bn. C.O. for training. Usual visit to Div. G.O.C.	
ARMENTIERES	11/10/15		Inspected St. Bridge Front Subsect. & inspectory Sector sup A.G.R. Bde R... (illegible)	

Instructions regarding War Diaries and Intelligence Summaries are contained in F. S. Regs., Part II. and the Staff Manual respectively. Title pages will be prepared in manuscript.

WAR DIARY
or
INTELLIGENCE SUMMARY.
(Erase heading not required.)

Army Form C. 2118

62

Place	Date	Hour	Summary of Events and Information	Remarks and references to Appendices
ARMENTIÈRES	13/11/15		Inspected [illegible] Front & Support lines with Capt. McQueen in morning. Visited [illegible] light installation at [illegible] CROIX [illegible], and 5th Div. [illegible] Park. Usual visit to Div. G.O.C. [illegible] of the [illegible] & [illegible] this afternoon.	
ARMENTIÈRES	14/11/15		Inspected bridges for 5" Howitzers also STAIN AVENUE & [illegible] Bridge, Front & Support lines, also GLOUCESTER AVENUE. Inspected [illegible] bridges in afternoon & arranged with G.O.C. [illegible] for working parties from 2 East Yorks Regt. Usual visit to Div G.O.C.	
ARMENTIÈRES	15/11/15		C.E. [illegible] Corps called & inspected 5th Div. & 2[illegible] Div. R.E. [illegible] & then inspected HOUPLINES work. In afternoon inspected works at CHAPELLE D'ARMENTIÈRES. Usual visit to Div G.O.C.	

WAR DIARY or INTELLIGENCE SUMMARY

Army Form C. 2118

Instructions regarding War Diaries and Intelligence Summaries are contained in F.S. Regs., Part II. and the Staff Manual respectively. Title pages will be prepared in manuscript.

(Erase heading not required.)

Place	Date	Hour	Summary of Events and Information	Remarks and references to Appendices
MONT ST ELOI	27/9/15		Orders also for M.G. Emplacements & for supporting points off LOTHIAN AVENUE on raising road. G HEAVY ACK 23 with Div. G.O.C. in reserve. 51st CHE 30th Div to be taking over in afternoon, inspected 15 Post, 50 Div & new communication and bridge close to Pt Bridge. Hoppé being moved by 1st Pg Ed B. Visit paid to Bde G.O.C. Capt. P.G. Queen 1st Lab. Inform RAMC Houses also B.ms.	
MONT ST ELOI	28/9/15		Time for the Offensive & Plan of same. Inst. Reports 15 Bn. P.I.G. for small Counter Attack. Then inspect defensive line in enemy's defenses of East of MONT ST ELOI & 51st Div. for first defensive front lines of our Guns.	
	29/9/15		Sent to Div to see commanding officer see second Right Hqr. that supports Infantry line & enemy attack. But for 7 & 8 artillery groups at FOURSIX, & DE RIVIÈRE, & ACHICOURT & and St.th G.T. Ques. ad at RIFLES Part Early Re. Supply HOUSE also. Went back to Bde G.O.C.	

Army Form C. 2118

WAR DIARY
or
INTELLIGENCE SUMMARY.

(Erase heading not required.)

Instructions regarding War Diaries and Intelligence Summaries are contained in F. S. Regs., Part II. and the Staff Manual respectively. Title pages will be prepared in manuscript.

H.Q. Air Staff Div.

Nov.

Vol. VII

131/763

SECRET

War Diary
of
C.R.E. 50th Division.

1st - 30th November 1915.

[signature] Lt. Col. RE
C.R.E. 50th Div.

Instructions regarding War Diaries and Intelligence Summaries are contained in F. S. Regs., Part II. and the Staff Manual respectively. Title pages will be prepared in manuscript.

WAR DIARY
or
INTELLIGENCE SUMMARY.
(Erase heading not required.)

Army Form C. 2118.

71

Place	Date	Hour	Summary of Events and Information	Remarks and references to Appendices
			Inspected Right & Centre Bdes. Drainage Schemes in morning.	
ARMENTIERES	7/9/15		Arranged details of work with C.R.E. 21st Div.	
			2nd [illegible] Fd. Co. R.E. relieved by 98th Fd. Co. R.E. 21st Div. Tonight.	
			[illegible] G.O.C.	
			Inspected Left Bde. Front, Support & Subsidiary lines. Trench 84 very wet.	
ARMENTIERES	8/9/15		Inspected Centre Machine Gun Emplacements along ARMENTIERES – [illegible] Ry., also damage [illegible] Permanent Bridge.	
			[illegible] G.O.C. Col. [illegible], C.R.E. 39th Div. arrived for instruction.	
ARMENTIERES	9/9/15		Took over C.E. [illegible] Corps, Gen. [illegible] & Col. [illegible] round Front & Support Trenches, Right Sector in morning.	
			Inspected [illegible] line & new field gun emplacement at HOUPLINES, and 2nd [illegible].	
			[illegible] G.O.C.	

Army Form C. 2118

WAR DIARY
or
INTELLIGENCE SUMMARY.

(Erase heading not required.)

Instructions regarding War Diaries and Intelligence Summaries are contained in F. S. Regs., Part II. and the Staff Manual respectively. Title pages will be prepared in manuscript.

Place	Date	Hour	Summary of Events and Information	Remarks and references to Appendices

WAR DIARY or INTELLIGENCE SUMMARY

Army Form C. 2118

73

Instructions regarding War Diaries and Intelligence Summaries are contained in F. S. Regs., Part II. and the Staff Manual respectively. Title pages will be prepared in manuscript.

(Erase heading not required.)

Place	Date	Hour	Summary of Events and Information	Remarks and references to Appendices
ARMENTIERES	13/11/15		Visited new Divl Hd Qrs at MERRIS from G.O.C. & went to HAZEBRUCK to see about getting trestles, called N.C.E.2nd Corps at BAILLEUL on way back. Inspected stock of fats at HOUPLINES in afternoon, found 1 officer & 2 sappers installed there of 2nd column to enter Transport Depot, in place of Tunnellers who were wounded.	
ARMENTIERES	14/11/15		Inspected new C.T. from CHAPELLE D'ARMENTIERES to wire of Subsidiary Line, also northern portion of 25 Divn Subsidiary line north of Ria 243. Inspected Subsidiary line of 23rd Divn, work of Lieut R280 in afternoon. 2 R.E. 2nd Divn called with regard to bridges & suppressing fronts.	
ARMENTIERES	15/11/15		Visited G.H.Q.2 line from PONT-DE-NIEPPE to ROMARIN, Vicos 111 & 78, Balby R.F.O. in morning. Inspected f. 2 North R.Co. Hope Line & RE Park in afternoon	

WAR DIARY
or
INTELLIGENCE SUMMARY.

(Erase heading not required.)

Army Form C. 2118

Instructions regarding War Diaries and Intelligence Summaries are contained in F. S. Regs. Part II. and the Staff Manual respectively. Title pages will be prepared in manuscript.

74

Place	Date	Hour	Summary of Events and Information	Remarks and references to Appendices
ARMENTIERES	16/11/15		Visited LILLE POST with Lt. Colonel Ht., C.W.E. 21st Div., Capt. Int. Queen, Adjutant 50th Div., the drainage system in morning. Attended Conference of C.R.E's at C.E's Office, BAILLEUL, at 2.30 p.m.	
ARMENTIERES	17/11/15		Visited LA CRECHE area in morning in connection with drainage plans. C.E. 2nd Army, Major-Gen. Glubb & C.E. 2nd Corps, Brig-Gen. Gorby, with L.C., Capt Levy came & viewed & inspected workshops etc. — Visited Hd. Qrs. 23rd Div., 3rd Corps, even later.	
ARMENTIERES	18/11/15		Visited 2nd South Lc. Co., then JAPAN ROAD and PLANK AVENUE, later PANAMA CANAL and HOUPLINES LOCK. BCR Artillery very active, and in shelling FORT. ESNARMONT with 9"× 12" Guns. Enemy retaliating on town. Visited 5th Div. Hd. Park & Workshops in afternoon	

Army Form C. 21

75

WAR DIARY
or
INTELLIGENCE SUMMARY.
(Erase heading not required.)

Place	Date	Hour	Summary of Events and Information	Remarks and references to Appendices
ARMENTIERES	19/11/15		Inspects Subsidiary Line with Col Coffin, C.R.E. 21st Div, Major Seymour, O.C. 7th Bn. G. Hds, Capt. Thwaites, O.C. 1 & 2 A.T. Cos., north of Rue d.S., with a view to commencing work the following day next. Inspects travel-foot-bridges in afternoon.	
ARMENTIERES	20/11/15		To BAILLEUL from C.E. re Subsidiary Line north of Rue d.S. — with Rainy to workshops and works premises in terry. Visits Garden, 15th Inf. Bde., in B.D. 16 b.o.6., then Div. H. Qrs. at MORRIS, arranged programme for construction of new Perrins 15th, 7th D.L.I. visits O.C. 7th D.L.I. at LA. ARCOT. In afternoon visits bridges.	
ARMENTIERES	21/11/15		Inspects Subsidiary line North of Rue d.S. with Capt. Roof, Queens in morning. Inspects LUNATIC LANE, BRICKYARD, AVENUE in afternoon. 2 o'clock F.G.M.E orders to entrain for CALAIS on Tuesday next.	

WAR DIARY
or
INTELLIGENCE SUMMARY.

Army Form C. 2118

76

Place	Date	Hour	Summary of Events and Information	Remarks and references to Appendices
ARMENTIERES	22/11/15		Inspected Salvaging Lines Report of Pain 293 & close various estes for correct location from Emplacements with O.C. 7" A.C. ; O.C. 63" A.T. G. H.S. Visited Pro. 50 Div. Park & Workshops.	
ARMENTIERES	23/11/15		Inspected Salvaging Lines Both of Pain 293 with C.E. 2" Corps in morning. Inspected ENATR LANE & new Right Emplacements at TISSAGE in afternoon.	
ARMENTIERES	24/11/15		Inspected Salvaging Lines Both of Pain 293 with Capt. S. Greene Rep. appt. N.50" Div. Second Lieut Confrennce. C.R.E. proceeded on leave.	
HOUBENTIERES	25/11/15		Visited Lt. McKenna RE at LA CREECHE & arranged for further men to be sent him for work in this area.	
PLOEGSTEERT	26/11/15		Visited work in trenches in Div. Rest Area & journey at NEUVILLE & gave orders for SD & LMs to 50" Div., 75" & 21" Div.	

Army Form C. 2118

WAR DIARY
or
INTELLIGENCE SUMMARY.
(Erase heading not required.)

Instructions regarding War Diaries and Intelligence Summaries are contained in F. S. Regs., Part II. and the Staff Manual respectively. Title pages will be prepared in manuscript.

77

Place	Date	Hour	Summary of Events and Information	Remarks and references to Appendices
ARMENTIERES	27/11/15		Inspection sites for both lines (2 required sites changed) - Site fixed for YMCA Hut at LA CRECHE.	
ARMENTIERES	28/11/15		Visited works in Rest area - fixed up sites for rest? Offr L. MORRIS - visited MORS BECUE re: supply of curtains -	
ARMENTIERES	29/11/15		Visited DWQ + Brig HdQrs 25. Various matters - The 921 Coy working under CRE returned -	
ARMENTIERES	30/11/15		Arrangs for trestle + visited YMCA tent - Visited L. Harrison 25. work in Rest area - Visited Div Park + HRS Horse Lines -	
ARMENTIERES	1/12/15		Despatches to Div Reps over of all latrines, cookhouses, Armory Shark compartrs - Proc. to YMCA tent sent over to STRAZEELE - issue of sheds etc: from HAZEBROUCK + distribution of NSC Logs + Mth Grd lection -	
ARMENTIERES	2/12/15		Visited Water tests with Capt Smith RE D. Offr - YMCA tent STRAZEELE - Water STEENWERCK STR. Sd-BURG - Handed over Rents 50th Div: area to Rents Officer BAILLEUL -	

J Wright Lt Col RE
C. R. E. 50 Div.

War Diary
of
C. R.E. 50th Division.

From 1/12/15 – 31/12/15.

[signature] Major
G. Cos. R.E.
C. R.E. 50 Div.

Vol VIII

Army Form C. 2118.

WAR DIARY
or
INTELLIGENCE SUMMARY.
(Erase heading not required.)

Instructions regarding War Diaries and Intelligence Summaries are contained in F. S. Regs., Part II. and the Staff Manual respectively. Title pages will be prepared in manuscript.

Place	Date	Hour	Summary of Events and Information	Remarks and references to Appendices
ARMENTIERES	1/12/15		Despatched to Div Rest Area reconnoitre of Labasée, Cerkeny Ballou & Harnes Huts Compak. Tender for Y.M.C.A. Hut and to STRAZEELE. Issue of huts received from HAZEBROUCK & despatched to A.S.C. H/Qrs & 1905 Vet Lehn.	
ARMENTIERES	2/12/15		Visited Bulk Huts with Capt Smith RE 2nd Corps., also Y.M.C.A. Hut at STRAZEELE & STEENWERCK. Handed over Huts 38 Div area to Rents' Officer, BAILLEUL.	
ARMENTIERES	3/12/15		Interviewed Kemp. sent to MERVILLE re delivery of stoves; first consignment promised by 9 Dec. Visited Trench 85 & mines with Lt Hutsputh R.E.	

Army Form C. 2118.

WAR DIARY
or
INTELLIGENCE SUMMARY.
(Erase heading not required.)

Instructions regarding War Diaries and Intelligence Summaries are contained in F. S. Regs., Part II. and the Staff Manual respectively. Title pages will be prepared in manuscript.

Place	Date	Hour	Summary of Events and Information	Remarks and references to Appendices
ARMENTIERES	4/12/15		C.R.A. returned from leave. Visited Div. H^d Qrs.; saw 2 sites of new Bath Houses in "rest" area, also Y.M.C.A. Hut & Tent. Visited Bath Conferences.	
ARMENTIERES	5/12/15		(Inspected) R.F.A. Gun Emplacements & Dug-outs at HOUPLINES, also SPRING & JAPAN AVENUES, very wet. To 38th Div. area in afternoon to see new Gun Pits.	
ARMENTIERES	6/12/15		Moved to new front. Corps H.Q. at Cassel, 50 Div. H placed to replace 50 Div. today. 7/6 Bde. arrived at 1.30 p.m. at MOTZE-BOUT, 15 & 2nd Both B. Co. & BAILLEUL, and march to PRADELLES. Left the Group made billeting arrangements. Visited C.R.A. 38th Div.	
CAESTRE	7/12/15		H^d Qrs Arty 50 Div. moved to CAESTRE today to replace 50 Div. Visited Div. G.O.C. in afternoon, and Major-General Fugge, G.O.C. 9 Division.	

Army Form C. 2118.

80

WAR DIARY
or
INTELLIGENCE SUMMARY.
(Erase heading not required.)

Instructions regarding War Diaries and Intelligence Summaries are contained in F. S. Regs., Part II. and the Staff Manual respectively. Title pages will be prepared in manuscript.

Place	Date	Hour	Summary of Events and Information	Remarks and references to Appendices
CAESTRE.	8/12/15		To HAZEBRUCK to see about trucks & carbines, with Capt. Pr. Queen Rl.	
CAESTRE	9/12/15		To MONT DE CHAT in afternoon.	
CAESTRE	10/12/15		To MERRIS & NOOTE BOOM to see Divl. G.O.C. & O.C. 7 Co. Rl. respectively. Thence to Billets of 1st Bn. Rl. Co. Rl.	
CAESTRE	11/12/15		To MERRIS to see Divl. G.O.C. & thence to Rd. Advanced Horse Park at STRAZEELE. To RENINGHELST with Capt. Prt Queen to see C.Rl. of Divn., U.C. C.Rl. Carpenter Rl. — made all arrangements for Rl. Co. of 9th to 50 Divn. to move on on Sunday next, 13 inst. — thence Rl. Park & ABEELE. Visited by O.C. 50 Divn. later on in day.	
CAESTRE	12/12/15		Visited G.O.C. 50 Divn. at MERRIS & O.C. 7 Co. Rl. O.C. 1 & 2 Bns. Rl. Co. called & saw arrangements about move.	

WAR DIARY or INTELLIGENCE SUMMARY

Army Form C. 2118.

Place	Date	Hour	Summary of Events and Information	Remarks and references to Appendices
CAESTRE 13/12/15			Three 7th Companies of 51st Div., disorganised by bus & conveyances by road, went to Div area at 5.0 a.m. in relief of 63rd Bde & 9th Bde Corps H.Q. 9th Div was ordered to CAESTRE & NOOTE-BOOM respectively. Capt. Butt Queens Rgt. went to C. pol. 9th Div took 9th Bay. Visited 51st Div. Q.O.C. in morning. In afternoon went to Bgo. 9th Bgo. & 510th Bde Hd. & BAILLEUL.	
CAESTRE 14/12/15			Col. Carpenter, C.M.S. 9th Div. took up his App., here today, with him & 57th Div. H. Bn. at MORRIS — in afternoon to Conference of C.M.S.s at C.E. 2nd Corps Office at BAILLEUL.	
RENINGHURST 15 O.R.S. M.M. 15/12/15			Spent hours rides — Visited 9th Div. H.Q. App. —	
16/12/15			Visited 3rd Bde. Appx, attached at H.15 B.4.9 and H.21 S.9.5, Grps 25 "Belgians" & Lanes. Also visited DICKEBUSHE and CANADA Hut.	

Army Form C. 2118.

82

WAR DIARY
or
INTELLIGENCE SUMMARY.
(Erase heading not required.)

Instructions regarding War Diaries and Intelligence Summaries are contained in F. S. Regs., Part II. and the Staff Manual respectively. Title pages will be prepared in manuscript.

Place	Date	Hour	Summary of Events and Information	Remarks and references to Appendices
	17/12/15		Visited CANADA HUTS, O.H.Q.3 Lini and Supporting Point H2, Latter in very bad condition after rain & requiring a lot of work.	
	18/12/15		Visited H.Q. "Dering's" at KRUISTRAAT. Went with George Pollard, D.C.O., O.C.'s North A Co. to Supporting Points Z a, b, c, and HB & HC; afterwards visited Major Gwyn Hd., O.C. 175 Tunnelling Co. H2. at VLAMERTINGHE.	
	19/12/15		Big "gas" attack early this morning on I Division north of Ypres; 3rd Div. left trenches east of ZILLEBEKE heavily shelled; Corps ordered I stand by but garrisons not got to be relieved. Visited Div. H2. etc.	
	20/12/15		Bishop of B. SUFFIE 18 g.m. 13 noon. Major C. B. Symes H2, O.C. 9.73. Co. R.E. wounded D.S.O.	
	21/12/15		Capt. H.E. Brown visited CANADA HUTS & their lines. C.R.E. called on Div. H2, etc. 3rd Div. 77th men were absent 10 a.m.	

Ypres 1 E route via POPERINGHE - PENINGHELST
Roads.

Army Form C. 2118.

G 3

WAR DIARY
or
INTELLIGENCE SUMMARY.
(Erase heading not required.)

Instructions regarding War Diaries and Intelligence Summaries are contained in F. S. Regs., Part II. and the Staff Manual respectively. Title pages will be prepared in manuscript.

Place	Date	Hour	Summary of Events and Information	Remarks and references to Appendices
RENINGHELST – POPERINGHE Road	22/12/15.		Visited Defended Localities, H¹ & H.K., also A.H.Q. 2 and Field Corps. Visited 50° Div. G.O.C. in afternoon.	
	23/12/15.		With Col. Harbaur, G.S.O. 1, 50° Div. to Defended Localities, H.Q. Mr. & G.H.Q. 2. H.Q. at above places. Div Reserve. Visited H¹ Div. 17° Div. & C.M.2. 17° Div. Visited 50° Div. F.O.C.	
	24/12/15.		Took R. Thompson, 7° D.O.E. on tour at KRUISSTRAAT in morning. Visited 150 Bays M¹ G.O. & 50° Div. H² Qrs.	
	25/12/15.		Major Cason Visited 175 Tunnelling Co. M. came to see me in morning – asked various questions met on relief of 9° Div. Visited by 5 Officers & 2/y men of 50° Div. Visited F.J. Co.	
	26/12/15.		Visited 121 Locts. From Line & Supports also Major Pollard & O.C. 1 Form. F. Co.	

Army Form C. 2118.

WAR DIARY
or
INTELLIGENCE SUMMARY.
(Erase heading not required.)

Instructions regarding War Diaries and Intelligence Summaries are contained in F.S. Regs., Part II. and the Staff Manual respectively. Title pages will be prepared in manuscript.

84

Place	Date	Hour	Summary of Events and Information	Remarks and references to Appendices
	27/12/15		Inspected DICKEBUSCH and CANADA Huts with Col. Vaux, A.C. 7 D.S.S. (Surveys) in morning. 50 Div. G.O.C. inspected Mt. Park in afternoon.	
	28/12/15.		With Capt. Mrs Green to 7° H.Q. Ms. & thus on with Lieut. Atkinson R.E. to inspect Left sector of Front Line, Vierstraat G.O.C. 138° Inf. Bnge. at Zinc & DEKS.	
	29/12/15		Inspected DICKEBUSCH and CANADA Huts with D.A.A. & Q.M.G. 50° Div. Visited R.O. H'Qrs, Div. H'Qrs. 50° Div.	
	30/12/15.		Inspected Centre Sector of Front Line with Major Burrup, 2° Norths. H.C. M.G. Lt. Col. Holdsen, G.S.O.I., 50° Div. called in afternoon.	
	31/12/15.		Visited 50° Div. H'Qrs. & thus C Mt., Ct. Gnd Mt., 17° Div. to arrange about Coys. moving tricks. Gen Petrie, C.E. 5° Corps called in afternoon. Belgian Interpreter arrived — Mr. Bempt, French Interpreter proceeded on leave.	

T.H.E. C, 27 b 3/5 — RENINGHELST - POPERINGHE Road.

E. W. T. Troup Lt. Col. R.E.
C.R.E. 50° Div

A.R. R.E. 30-A Das
Jan
Vol IX

Army Form C. 2118.
85

WAR DIARY
or
INTELLIGENCE SUMMARY.
(Erase heading not required.)

Place	Date	Hour	Summary of Events and Information	Remarks and references to Appendices
	1/1/16.		Visited party of Entrenching Bn. at work at KRUISSTRAAT, also Mt. Dump Mine & G.O.C. 153 Bde. with Capt. G & E. Queen Mt. 2 Lieut. Spiritt Mt. J.Co. res. to Hospital with shrapnel wound in toe. Visited F.A. Ambulance in afternoon.	
	2/1/16.		Reconnoitred country near LARCHWOOD HUTS for Div. Staff; Visited I.B & Bridges on Canal, also working party of 2" Entrenching Bn.	
	3/1/16.		Inspected DICKEBUSCH and CANADA HUTS, also Hq & Ho & and 50" Div. G.O.C. Visited 50" Div. Hd Qrs. in afternoon.	
	4/1/16.		With Capt. G & E. Queen, Visited 150" Bde., and Front Trenches of Left Sector, also RAILWAY DUGOUTS and 150" Bde. Hd. Qrs.	

Frame 1/2 miles E. POPERINGHE - RENINGHELST Rd.

WAR DIARY or INTELLIGENCE SUMMARY

Army Form C. 2118.

(Erase heading not required.)

Instructions regarding War Diaries and Intelligence Summaries are contained in F. S. Regs., Part II. and the Staff Manual respectively. Title pages will be prepared in manuscript.

Place: **Forms 1'C ouths as POPERINGHE-RENINGHERST Road.**

Date	Hour	Summary of Events and Information	Remarks and references to Appendices
5/1/16		Saw Divl. G.O.C. with reference to providing accommodation for Support Coy. when the Line is held by 2 Brigades only — own H.Qy. Commanders in some outpost.	
6/1/16		Visited O.C. 1st Suffk. R.A. & then to KRUISSTAART, ZILLEBEKE and RAILWAY DUG OUTS to settle various matters; Brig-Genl. Pepir, C.E. 5' Corps called to see Mr. Park.	Lieut-Col. C.B. Smyth D.S.O. ↔ Capt. R. J. A. McQueen "Unations" in September 1st Jany 1916
7/1/16		To Front Line, KRISAAH & SQUARE WOODS with Col. Holdens, G.S.O.I. 5° Div.	
8/1/16		To 1st Su.R. H.Q. Ill. & then visited H.B., H.O. Hg., DICKEBUSCH HUTS in morning. Visited Divl. H.Q. Gen. O'Gov in afternoon.	
9/1/16		Was taken the Queen to RAILWAY DUGOUTS & Fd. Section of Front Line — heavy bombardment of Hill 60. Enemy retaliated on BEDFORD HOUSE	

Army Form C. 2118.

WAR DIARY
or
INTELLIGENCE SUMMARY.
(Erase heading not required.)

Instructions regarding War Diaries and Intelligence Summaries are contained in F. S. Regs., Part II. and the Staff Manual respectively. Title pages will be prepared in manuscript.

67

Place	Date	Hour	Summary of Events and Information	Remarks and references to Appendices
From 1½ miles on POPPERINGHE - RENINGHELST Rd.	10/1/16.		Inspected SCOTTISH·LINES·HUTS in morning. Visited Divl. 50th Hd Qrs. in afternoon.	
	11/1/16.		With Major Cowan RE., O.C. 175th Tunnelling Co R.E. to visit Mines in Trench 84 - Visited 157th Bde. Hd Qrs., R.6 etc. in morng.	
	12/1/16.		Visited H2 & H3, also DICKEBUSCH·HUTS in morning. Carried out experiments with "Tub" Br. G. Engsee. in afternoon - Col. Holdern, G.V.O.I. 50th Div. called.	
	13/1/16.		With Capt. McQueen R.H.B. & H.C. down to SUNKEN·ROAD, S.47, S.48, MANOR·FARM and RAILWAY·DUGOUTS.	
	14/1/16.		Inspected Footplate Locations, H2 and H3, with Capt. Thomson, J.D.of.S. (Winters) & called on what work should be done. Major Cowan, O.C. 175 Tunnelling Co R.E. and Col. Thurston, A.D.M.S. 50th Div. called in afternoon.	

2353 Wt. W2344/1454 700,000 5/15 D. D. & L. A.D.S.S. Forms/C 2118.

Army Form C. 2118.

WAR DIARY
or
INTELLIGENCE SUMMARY.
(Erase heading not required.)

Instructions regarding War Diaries and Intelligence Summaries are contained in F. S. Regs., Part II. and the Staff Manual respectively. Title pages will be prepared in manuscript.

Place	Date	Hour	Summary of Events and Information	Remarks and references to Appendices
	15/1/16		Visited DICKEBUSCH HUTS, H² & H² with Capt. R² & Greer H². Visited Div. H⁴ & Bro. & experimented with new M.G. Emp² accessories.	
	16/1/16		C.R.A. 2n² Division spent day learning all he could in workshops etc in morning & saw 1ˢᵗ South Af. G. Artillery in afternoon. Visited 50 Div. G.O.C.	
	17/1/16		Inspected H², H.R. & H² in morning. Visited 50 Div. H² Bro.	
	18/1/16		Experiments in H² Parth with new M.G. Emp² accessories. Went with Col. Ihart, G.S.O.2, 50 Div. to see Philippo via Canal, RAILWAY DUGOUTS, FOSSE WAY & MANOR FARM.	
	19/1/16		Inspected H², H² & H.R. & DICKEBUSCH HUTS in morning. Gen. Petrie, C.R.E. 5 Corps, called in afternoon. Visited 50 Div. H² Bro.	

Army Form C. 2118.

WAR DIARY
or
INTELLIGENCE SUMMARY.
(Erase heading not required.)

Instructions regarding War Diaries and Intelligence Summaries are contained in F. S. Regs., Part II. and the Staff Manual respectively. Title pages will be prepared in manuscript.

Place	Date	Hour	Summary of Events and Information	Remarks and references to Appendices
	20/1/16		Visited 1st Inth. H.Q. H.E., also KRUISTRAAT Dumps, SWAN CHATEAU, H.Q. H.E., RAILWAY DUGOUTS, MANOR FARM, ARMAGH WOOD.	
	21/1/16		Inspected H.Q. H.E. & CANADA HUTS. Visited 50th Div. D.H.Q.	
	22/1/16		Inspected H.Q. & H.E., also DICKEBUSCH HUTS in morning. Visited 50th Div. D.H.Q.	
	23/1/16		Inspected Left Bdge. Front Trenches with Capt. McQueen, O.C. 7 G.H.E., also returns for holding forlorn outp of Front Line.	
	24/1/16		Inspected SCOTTISH LINES in morning — visited 50th Div. G.O.C. in afternoon.	
	25/1/16		Visited Rd. Schn. Front Line & Dug-Outs in ARMAGH WOOD with Major Pollard, O.C. 1st Wilth. H. Co. H.E., who was wounded by a sniper.	

Army Form C. 2118.

90.

WAR DIARY
or
INTELLIGENCE SUMMARY.
(Erase heading not required.)

Instructions regarding War Diaries and Intelligence Summaries are contained in F. S. Regs., Part II. and the Staff Manual respectively. Title pages will be prepared in manuscript.

Place	Date	Hour	Summary of Events and Information	Remarks and references to Appendices
B.Well 1½ mile on POPERINGHE - RENINGHELST Rd.	26/1/16.		Attended monthly "Water Board" Committee at 50th Div. Hd Qrs. — Carried out experiments with "toc" M.G. Emplacement.	
	27/1/16.		Inspected KRUISTRAAT. DUMP, 157th Hd Qrs., RAILWAY. DUGOUTS, H2, H6 + H9.	Major G.C. Williams, D.S.o. O.C. 1st Batln. A.C.M.S. assumed, 25/1/16
	28/1/16.		Attended Conference of Brigadiers & G.O.C. at Adv. D.H.Q. in morning on various defensive localities in front lines. Inspected SCOTTISH. LINES in afternoon.	
	29/1/16.		Inspected DICKEBUSCH. HUTS, H3, H6, H4, H5 + H7. Visited 51st Div. Hd Qrs.	
	30/1/16.		Attended Conference at 50th Div. Hd Qrs. on "Tunnelling" with G.O.C. & O.C. 175 Tunnelling Co. N.E. Visited 79 Co. in afternoon.	

Army Form C. 2118.

WAR DIARY
or
INTELLIGENCE SUMMARY.
(Erase heading not required.)

Place	Date	Hour	Summary of Events and Information	Remarks and references to Appendices
	3/1/16.		To ZILLEBEKE DUGOUTS, H⁴ Coy. 137 Inf. Bde. — went round Left sector with H.O.C. 137 Inf. Bde. & relieved various points. Inspects RAILWAY DUGOUTS. W. Nunn R.A.M.C. C.M.O. 46 Div.	

Form, ½ mile on RENINGHELST - POPPERINGHE Road.

Original.

War Diary

C.R.E. 50th Division.

From Feb. 1st 1916
To Feb. 29th 1916.

C.L. Singer
Lt. Col. R.E.
C.R.E. 50th Div.

H.Q. R.E. 50 Div / Feb / 8vol X

Army Form C. 2118.

g 2

WAR DIARY
or
INTELLIGENCE SUMMARY.
(Erase heading not required.)

Place	Date	Hour	Summary of Events and Information	Remarks and references to Appendices
	1/2/16.		Inspected KRUISSTRAAT·DUMP, Advanced D.H.Q., RAILWAY. DUGOUTS in morning, also H.Q. Visited 50' Div. H.Q. Qrs. in afternoon.	
	2/2/16.		Inspected DICKEBUSCH·HUTS & chow arks for water-supply return — visited parties working at Ho, Hq and H.R. Inspected CANADA·HUTS. Gen. Perkin, C.E. 5' Corps called.	
	3/2/16.		Saw O.C. 175 Tunnelling Co. Mt. with reference to Underground Shelters in Zout Zavi — inspected RAILWAY·DUGOUTS, road from Bridge 16 to SHRAPNEL·CORNER, Pet Dump, KRUISSTRAAT. Visited 5' Div. G.O.C.	
	4/2/16.		Visited DICKEBUSCH·HUTS in morning — new railway in afternoon.	

Army Form C. 2118.

WAR DIARY
or
INTELLIGENCE SUMMARY.
(Erase heading not required.)

93

Place	Date	Hour	Summary of Events and Information	Remarks and references to Appendices
	5/2/16		Inspected Grenade School at DICKEBUSCH HUTS, also HH. HQ. Visited F. C. 1st Irish Fd. Co. Ticks. Visited 50' Div. Hd Qrs.	
	6/2/16.		Attended a Conference at Adv. D.H.Q. of G.O.C. 50° Div., 3 Brigadiers & O.C. 175 Tunnelling Co. Rl. Inspects Rl. Dumps, KRUISTRAAT. Visited A.D.M.S. 50' Div. Re "Gas" Buy-out.	
	7/2/16.		Visited DICKEBUSCH HUTS & their new Rifle Range at SCOTTISH LINES with 50' Div. G.O.C. Visited 50' Div. Hd Qrs.	
	8/2/16.		Visited Supp Hutts And Trenches with G.O.C. 50' Div. & G.O.C. 157 Inf. Bde - opened various points in front turns.	
	9/2/16.		Inspected Hq, MP. & Hi. Visited Fd. Co. - inspected new water supply at DICKEBUSCH HUTS. Visited 50' Div. G.O.C.	

From 1/2 entre in POPERINGHE - KENINGHELST Road.

Army Form C. 2118.

94.

WAR DIARY
or
INTELLIGENCE SUMMARY.
(Erase heading not required.)

Place	Date	Hour	Summary of Events and Information	Remarks and references to Appendices
	10/2/16		To Front Line — chose sites for 2 Machine Gun Emplacements at SWAN CHATEAU. Then inspected Road to Bridge 18, RAILWAY DUGOUTS, MANOR FARM & ZILLEBEKE, also Div. Adv. H⁺ Qrs.	
	11/2/16		Inspected water supply at DICKEBUSCH HUTS.	
	12/2/16		Inspected H.Q. & H⁺, also DICKEBUSCH HUTS water supply — saw O.C. 7 F. Co. R.E. Visited 50ᵗʰ Div. H⁺ Qrs.	
	13/2/16		Visited 50ᵗʰ Div. H⁺ Qrs. in morning. Adjt. to BAILLEULCR. & Hqs various Bdes.	
	14/2/16		Attended a Conference at Adv. D.H.Q. with G.O.C. & Brigadiers, also O.C. 175 Tunnelling Co. R.E. Visited 50ᵗʰ Div. H⁺ Qrs. in afternoon. Heavy shelling of R.E. Dumps, KRUISTRAAT- Grenade Bomb set on fire.	
	15/2/16		Visited 50ᵗʰ Div. H⁺ Qrs. & then KRUISTRAAT in morning with D.A.A. & Q.M.G. 2 of 50ᵗʰ Div.	

WAR DIARY or INTELLIGENCE SUMMARY

Army Form C. 2118.

95

Place	Date	Hour	Summary of Events and Information	Remarks and references to Appendices
	16/9/16		Major General Glubb, C.E. 2nd Army, visited here - together we inspected 9" & 2"Welsh Fd. Cos. Billets - I had myself slightly inspected last night. Visited 57th Divn. H? Qrs.	
	17/9/16		Visited PRUINSTRAAT DUMP, MANOR FARM, ZILLEBEKE, RAILWAY DUGOUTS, then inspected road from SHRAPNEL CORNER to BELLEGOED FARM.	
	18/9/16		Visited 3 Brigade H? Qrs. with Lt. Col. Heward, G.S.O.I, 50th Divn., then visited front trenches 49, 50, A1, A1, 35 & 37. Attended conference at Divl. H? Qrs. of G.O.C., 3 Brigadiers, O.C. 175 Tunnelling Co R.E. & O.C Trench Mortar Battery.	
	19/9/16		Visited 50th Divn. H? Qrs. 3 Zeppelins reported to have crossed SANCTUARY WOOD about 5 a.m. flying East.	
	20/9/16		Hostile aeroplane raid on POPERINGHE last night & this morning.	

Bomb 1½ miles N. of RENINGHELST & 1/2 a POPERINGHE Rd.

Army Form C. 2118.

96

WAR DIARY
or
INTELLIGENCE SUMMARY.
(Erase heading not required.)

From 1½ miles on RENINGHELST Road, G.27.b

Place	Date	Hour	Summary of Events and Information	Remarks and references to Appendices
	21/2/16.		Visited 50th Div. Hd Qrs. Heavy shelling all day, partially with gas shells.	
	22/2/16.		Attended Conference at Adv. Hd Qrs. with G.O.C. 50 Div, Brigadier, G.O.C. R.A., O.C. Tunnelling Coy R.E., G.O.C.R.A., O.C. Trench Mortar Battery. Inspected A.H.Q. 2nd Divn with G.O.C.R.E.	
	23/2/16.		Visited DICKEBUSCH and Hd in morning. Instructed party of T.D.C.S. (Pioneers) in laying out dummy trenches.	
	24/2/16.		Visited N.Z. Decamp KRUISSTRAAT, H3, H0, H2, H0, DICKEBUSCH HUTS water supply - also fire Coy billets.	
	25/2/16.		Visited CANADA HUTS in morning. Attended at 50 Div. H.Q. in afternoon.	
	26/2/16.		Attended Conference at Adv. D.H.Q. with G.O.C., Brigadier, G.O.C.R.A., O.C. Tunnelling Co. R.E. and O.C. Trench Mortars. Witnessed Smoke Bomb experiments. Visited Div. H.Q. in afternoon.	

Army Form C. 2118.

97

WAR DIARY
or
INTELLIGENCE SUMMARY.
(Erase heading not required.)

Farm, G.27.b, on RENINGHELT - POPERINGHE Road.

Place	Date	Hour	Summary of Events and Information	Remarks and references to Appendices
	27/3/16		Reconnoitred C.H. & 2 Lins with 3 Mk. & 2 Divnl. Officers & decided on details of giving up front from BELLEGARDE FARM to CANAL.	
	28/3/16		Capt. Howell visited D.H.Q. and QUINTON. Riding from me. Gen. Pétain, C.E. 5° Corps called to see me.	
	29/3/16		Visited G.H.Q. 2° Lini, KRUISTRAAT, Div. Advanced H.Q. etc. Visited D.H.Q. in afternoon.	

C L Nugent M. Col. M.
C.R.E. 50° Div.

Original

War Diary
of
C.R.E. 50th Division.

from 1st March 1916
to 31st March 1916.

Vol XI

[signature]
Lt Col. R.E.
C.R.E. 50th Div

Army Form C. 2118.

98.

WAR DIARY
or
INTELLIGENCE SUMMARY.
(Erase heading not required.)

Instructions regarding War Diaries and Intelligence Summaries are contained in F.S. Regs., Part II. and the Staff Manual respectively. Title pages will be prepared in manuscript.

Place	Date	Hour	Summary of Events and Information	Remarks and references to Appendices
	1/3/16		Inspected DCKE BUSCHE. HUTS, Water Supply, M.G. Coy. Camps, H.Q. & H.Q. & A. Coy. billets. Visited Div. H.Q. also.	
	2/3/16		Inspected R.H.Q. 2 Line & reconnoitred position for proposed new road with Capt. Wilkinson, R.A.R.E. Saw a batch of German prisoners taken by 17 Div. East night. Attended Conference at D.H.Q. of G.O.C. & Gen. Gaselee, C.E. 2 Army.	
	3/3/16		O.C. 4 Prov in the Sept. Coy.R.E. came about taking over Methuselah's Lines. agreed to this & visited Lines in morning. O.C. 2 Entrenching Bn. also called re working parties. Visited G.O.C. 50 Div.	
	4/3/16		Inspected new billets of 175 Tunnelling Co. R.E. Visited G.O.C. 50 Div.	

2353 Wt. W2514/1454 700,000 5/15 D.D. & L. A.D.S.S. Forms/C. 2118.

WAR DIARY
or
INTELLIGENCE SUMMARY.
(Erase heading not required.)

Army Form C. 2118.

99

Instructions regarding War Diaries and Intelligence Summaries are contained in F. S. Regs., Part II. and the Staff Manual respectively. Title pages will be prepared in manuscript.

Place	Date	Hour	Summary of Events and Information	Remarks and references to Appendices
	5/3/16		Visited the 3 Field Coys. Their unexpected having of G.H.Q.2 Line & communication trenches for two long communication trenches back from this line. Inspired road from CARREFOUR CORNER to RAILWAY DUGOUTS & the new ground thus there etc.	
	6/3/16		Close ride at Railway Cutting with O.C. 175 Tunnelling Co. R.E. and G.S.O.3. Then arranged with O.C. 1st South Fd. Co. as to crews way across cutting & for necessary working parties.	
	7/3/16		Visited Lt. Col. Craven M.C., C.R.E. 20 Division about arrangements for his 104th Fd. Co. to relieve my 1 Fd. Co. Allotment Conference of G.O.C., Brigadiers, C.R.A. & G.S.O.1 at Corps D.H.Q.	
	8/3/16		Handed over Staff Ridge stocks to C.R.E. 20 Division. Took him all round it. Visited D.H.Q. in evening.	
	9/3/16		Visited Fd. Coys. to arrange new work — and G.S.O.2 & Bdgr. M.S. officer, 149 Bdgr. at A&r. D.H.Q. Then visited Fd. Coys. again.	

Form G.27.2. Sheet 28. D.W. RENINGHELST - POPERINGHE Road.

Army Form C. 2118.

100

WAR DIARY
or
INTELLIGENCE SUMMARY.
(Erase heading not required.)

Instructions regarding War Diaries and Intelligence Summaries are contained in F. S. Regs., Part II. and the Staff Manual respectively. Title pages will be prepared in manuscript.

Farm G.27.b ~ RENINGHELST - POPPERINGHE Road.

Place	Date	Hour	Summary of Events and Information	Remarks and references to Appendices
	10/3/16		Visited 3 F. Cos. with reference to special work of last night, inspected the lining of G.H.Q. 2nd Line. French Tramway from Mt. Dump. NR VI/STRAAT. Visited 50th Div. H4 Qrs.	
	11/3/16		Inspected special work in Right after seeing 3 F. Cos. — Visited 50th Div. H4 Qrs. & attended a Conference of Div. G.O.C.'s with Corps Commdr. at 2 P.M. GSE.E.	
	12/3/16		Visited three F. Cos. & inspected G.H.Q. 2nd Line. Visited Cornwall A.T. Coys Workshops at ABEELE & inspected types of Light Bridges for crossing trenches for Inf. & Cav. Visited 50th Div. H4 Qrs.	
	13/3/16		To 50th Div. H4 Qrs. & then to 2nd Canadian Div. H4 Qrs. at WESTOUTRE to see C. R.E.'s Bridges, rock etc... Lt Col Hughes — all round satisfactory. To Southampton Lines later.	
	14/3/16		Visited 3 F. Cos. three upto L Grand Bois to inspect special work done lately. Visited 50th Div. H4 Qrs.	

Army Form C. 2118.

WAR DIARY
or
INTELLIGENCE SUMMARY.
(Erase heading not required.)

Instructions regarding War Diaries and Intelligence Summaries are contained in F. S. Regs., Part II. and the Staff Manual respectively. Title pages will be prepared in manuscript.

107

Place	Date	Hour	Summary of Events and Information	Remarks and references to Appendices
Farm G.27.b. Shut 28. Ow RENINGHELST - POPERINGHE Rd.	15/3/16		Visited Mess Fd. Coys., DICKEBUSCH HUTS and Water Supply. Visited 50' Div. Hd. Qrs. — C.R.E. 1st Canadian Div. came to see me with reference to erection of huts.	
	16/3/16		To KRUISSTRAAT, inspected new M.G. Cupolas at I.9 & settled on wiring in front of G.H.Q 2 Line with 2nd Lieut. BRADLEY, 7.D.L.9. (Pervince). Visited 50' Div. Hd. Qrs.	
	17/3/16		Visited 3 Fd. Coys. & New DICKEBUSCH HUTS: Forthfied localities at HX & HY. Visited 50' Div. Hd. Qrs.	
	18/3/16		Visited Fd. Coys. & 175 Tunnelling Co. Hd. — met Controller of Mines, & Lt. Col. Thomson RE. Visited 50' Div. Hd. Qrs.	
	19/3/16		Visited 2nd North. Fd. Co. & New G.H.Q. 2nd Line, JOHNSTONE'S TRENCH RAILWAY CUTTING, and road from SHARPNEL CORNER to ZILLEBEKE STATION. Visited 50' Div. Hd. Qrs.	

Army Form C. 2118.

102

WAR DIARY
or
INTELLIGENCE SUMMARY.
(Erase heading not required.)

Instructions regarding War Diaries and Intelligence Summaries are contained in F. S. Regs., Part II. and the Staff Manual respectively. Title pages will be prepared in manuscript.

Place	Date	Hour	Summary of Events and Information	Remarks and references to Appendices
	20/3/16		C.E.S. Corps called & took me to select site for new railway siding & R.E. Yard near LA CLYTTE – Visited C.R.E.'s of 3rd & 2nd Divisions. Visited 50 Div. Hd. Qrs.	
	21/3/16		Took Major McFaile, C.R.E. 2nd Canadian Div. to KRUISSTRAAT & Fd. Coys Billets. Visited 50 Div. Hd. Qrs.	
	22/3/16		Inspected water supply DICKEBUSCH HUTS & visited Col. Vaux, O.C. 1 D.L.I. (Pioneers). Visited 50 Div. Hd. Qrs.	
	23/3/16		Took C.R.E. 1st Canadian Division up to RAILWAY CUTTING, SHRAPNEL CORNER, TRANSPORT FARM etc.	
	24/3/16		Visited 3 Field Coys. & DICKEBUSCH HUTS. Visited 50 Div. Hd Qrs.	

2353 Wt. W3514/1451 750,000 5/15 D. D. & L. A.D.S.S. Forms/C 2118.

Army Form C. 2118.

103

WAR DIARY
or
INTELLIGENCE SUMMARY.
(Erase heading not required.)

Instructions regarding War Diaries and Intelligence Summaries are contained in F. S. Regs., Part II. and the Staff Manual respectively. Title pages will be prepared in manuscript.

Place	Date	Hour	Summary of Events and Information	Remarks and references to Appendices
	25/3/16		Visited 3 Fiel Coys. & H⁴ Qrs. 153ʳᵈ Inf. Bde.	
			Visited 51ˢᵗ Div. H⁴ Qrs. - C.R.E., Lt. Cl. Anderson, Com. R.E., also O.C. 253 Tunnelling Co. Re. conc. & report.	
	26/3/16		Visited new Bivou. of 3 Fd. Coys. with Adjutant, Capt. Norell, in morning.	
			Called in at H⁴ Qrs. 60 Div.	
	27/3/16		Visited Fd. Coys., Tunnelling Co. 175, KRUISTRAAT.	
			Called at 50 Div. H⁴ Qrs. & went to SCHERPENBURGH with G.O.C.	
	28/3/16		Saw 2ⁿᵈ In.R. Fd. Co. R.E. march out to "Rest" Area. Went up to A.C.H. & 2 Fds. Dire. LILLE ROAD.	
			LANGHOF CHATEAUX.	
			Visited 50 Div. H⁴ Qrs. Capt. Pate Queen, O.C. 7 Fd. G. Conc. & see me.	
	29/3/16		Visited C.R.E. III. Division & arranged various matters.	
			Called on 57 Div. H⁴ Qrs.	

Jeans, G. 27.3 (March 28) on RENINGHELST-POPERINGE Road.

Army Form C. 2118.

WAR DIARY
or
INTELLIGENCE SUMMARY.
(Erase heading not required.)

104

Place	Date	Hour	Summary of Events and Information	Remarks and references to Appendices
	30/3/16		Visited F. Coys. about mines. Also C.R.E. 2nd Canadian Div. at WESTOUTRE. Called on 50th Div. H'Qrs. O.C. 175 Tunnelling Co. came to see me – Capt. Carlisle M.C. 2nd N. Mid. F.C. R.E. moved to LOCRE H of F Farm today.	
	31/3/16		Went over Rd. Bridge (137th Inf. Bdge.) Sector with C.E. 2nd Army, Major-General Glubb K.E. & O.C. 2nd F. Co. R.E. (Capt. Int. Queen M.E.).	

C.R.E. 50th Div.

From G.27.b at RENINGHELST - POPERINGHE Rd.

SECRET

Original

War Diary
of
C.R.E. 50th Division
from 1st April 1916
to 30th April 1916.

[stamp: C.R.E. No. 2543 30 APR 1916 50th DIVISION]

C.W. Singer
Lt. Col. R.E.
C.R.E. 50th Div.

Army Form C. 2118.

WAR DIARY
or
INTELLIGENCE SUMMARY.
(Erase heading not required.)

105.

Place	Date	Hour	Summary of Events and Information	Remarks and references to Appendices
LOCRE G.7.7.b	1/4/16		Inspected 1st Mock. F.A. Co. marching with 149th Inf. Bde. to Canadian Rest area — visited	
KEMMELHOF			O.C. 253rd Tunnelling Co. R.E., Major Griffin R.E. at LA CLYTTE & New C.P. of 2nd Canadian Div.	
POPERINGHE RD.			at WESTOUTRE. Visited 50th Div. H.Q. Also	
WESTOUTRE	2/4/16		Moved billets today. Visited 1st Entrenching Bn. & arranged work for them. Visited 2nd Sth.	
			Fd. Co. R.E. & went over Ad. Hdqrs. (150) sector of front trenches.	
			1st North Md. Co. moved to R.E. FARM, N.15.c.3/4. Visited 28th S. W. Today.	
do.	3/4/16		Visited clearing dams at 10,13,&2 units Fd. Officers of 1st Entrenching Bn. — Visited 1st South	
			Fd. Co. at R.E. Farm, then walked over to inspect the subsidiary & G.H.Q. 2nd Line.	
			Visited Div. H.Q. Also.	
do.	4/4/16		Inspected G.H.Q. 2nd Line from Left to LINDENHOEK & Subsidiary Line — Ground good in places, but	
			studded. Visited fields on MONT RUGE & 50th Div. H.Qrs. 1st Fd. Co. R.E. marches into billets of	
do.	5/4/16		Inspected KEMMEL DEFENCES with G.O.C. 50th Div.	
			Inspected WESTOUTRE trenches & Laundry with adjacent Fit.	

Army Form C. 2118.

WAR DIARY
or
INTELLIGENCE SUMMARY.
(Erase heading not required.)

Instructions regarding War Diaries and Intelligence Summaries are contained in F. S. Regs., Part II. and the Staff Manual respectively. Title pages will be prepared in manuscript.

Place	Date	Hour	Summary of Events and Information	Remarks and references to Appendices
WESTOUTRE.	6/4/16.		Inspected Saboraty Line with G.O.C. 50th Div.	
"	7/4/16.		Visited SCHERPENBERG DEFENCES – attended meeting of DivG.O.C.s Brigadiers, C.R.A. etc.	
"	8/4/16.		Visited 7th & 1st Nth. Md. Co. M.R., also 5th Labour Bn. & 1st Entrenching Bn. at VIERSTRAAT's orders. Inspected water supply.	
"	9/4/16.		Inspected SCHERPENBERG DEFENCES & arranged for work in them with 1st Entrenching Bn. and F.S.O.s. (Pioneers).	
"	9/4/16.		Attended Water Meeting at 5th Corps Hd Qrs. – inspected water supply.	
"	10/4/16.		With Lt. Col. Stuart, G.S.O. I, 50th Div. to 149th Inf. Bde. Hd Qrs. & then inspected Rest Bergode section & details on what programme to work on.	
"	11/4/16.		Visited 1/1 East Riding Fd. Co., 7th Fd. Co. & 1st D.L.I. (Pioneers) with reference to work. Chose site for alarm near LA CLYTTE-KEMMEL Road with Capt. Br.S. General Nth., Inspected water supply at KEMMEL.	

Army Form C. 2118.

107.

WAR DIARY
or
INTELLIGENCE SUMMARY.
(Erase heading not required.)

Instructions regarding War Diaries and Intelligence Summaries are contained in F. S. Regs., Part II. and the Staff Manual respectively. Title pages will be prepared in manuscript.

Place	Date	Hour	Summary of Events and Information	Remarks and references to Appendices
WESTOUTRE.	12/4/16		Walked to see 2nd North Fd. Co. at LOCREHOF — O.C. 1st Entrenching Mnrs. reported called about work. Visited 50' Div. G.O.C.	
"	13/4/16		To see C.E. 5th Corps at BAILLEUL & then C. R.E. 3rd Div. at FLETRE. O.C. 1/1 East Riding Fd. Co. & O.C. 6 Canadian Fd. Co. called. Chose site for plans for water supply at 17.15.2. with 2.Lt. Busby R.E. 1st North Fd. Co. R.E. P.M. Rennell Fd personal to 2 Lieut. Ht.	
"	14/4/16		Went all round the Div. Front with Lt. A. Stuart, G.S.O.I. 50' Div. & the G.S.O.I of 3rd Div.	
"	15/4/16		Inspected water supply for front trenches at KEMMEL Hill with O.C. 2 North Fd. Co. & visited 1 & 1st North. Fd. Co. Inspected water supply in MONT ROUGE.	
"	16/4/16		C.R.E. 3rd Div. called — selected sites for new water supplies with O.C. 7 Fd. Co. Attended meeting at Div. Hd. Qrs. of Brigadiers of 3rd & 50' Div. to settle on programme of work.	

Army Form C. 2118.

108.

WAR DIARY
or
INTELLIGENCE SUMMARY.

(Erase heading not required.)

Instructions regarding War Diaries and Intelligence Summaries are contained in F. S. Regs., Part II. and the Staff Manual respectively. Title pages will be prepared in manuscript.

Place	Date	Hour	Summary of Events and Information	Remarks and references to Appendices
WESTOUTRE.	17/4/16		Inspected new Grenade School at SCHERPENBERG & new work in VIERSTRAAT SWITCH. Inspected new water supply for part of MONT ROUGE.	
"	18/4/16		Took Lt. Col. Elliot, C.M.E. 3rd Div, over all back works. Visited 1st & 2nd Irish F. Co. Visited Laundry & Hd. Qrs. 50th Div.	
"	19/4/16		Took A.S.O.I., Lt. Col. De Buell & C.M.E. 3rd Div. round front & communication trenches of Right & Centre Brigades.	
"	20/4/16		Inspected new trench at LOCRE & acted orders for three lines etc. with Capt. Stowell M.E. Adjutant M.E. 50th Div.	
"	21/4/16		Office work only. Afternoon Searching at 52nd Div. Hd. Qrs. of Brigadiers & divisional arrangements for training while in rest area.	
"	22/4/16		Adjutant M.E. visited FLÊTRE & 2nd Army Workshops. 7th F.A.C. marched to Rest Area to R.13.2. (Sheet 27).	

Army Form C. 2118.

109

WAR DIARY
or
INTELLIGENCE SUMMARY.
(Erase heading not required.)

Instructions regarding War Diaries and Intelligence Summaries are contained in F. S. Regs., Part II. and the Staff Manual respectively. Title pages will be prepared in manuscript.

Place	Date	Hour	Summary of Events and Information	Remarks and references to Appendices
WESTOUTRE	23/4/16		Visited 7" D.L.I. (Pioneers) to arrange about work in VIERSTRAAT SWITCH – Then on to C.E. 5" Corps, C. Rl. 3" Division and O.C. 7" F. Co. at new billet. Visits to Div. H"rs.	
"	24/4/16		Visited 7" D.L.I. (Pioneers) & 1" North. Fd. Co. to arrange work – inspected water supply at KEMMEL & also in LA-CLYTTE Road. Inspected Water Supply at WESTOUTRE and in neighbourhood.	
FLETRE	25/4/16		Handed over to C.R.E. 3rd Div. & moved to LA-CLYTTE today with 7" D.T.J. (Pioneers) for work in VIERSTRAAT SWITCH. Visits 7" Fd. Co.	
"	26/4/16		Visited H"rs 50" Div. – also H"rs 151 Inf. Bdge. Took Capt. McQueen over VIERSTRAAT. Turned after dark.	
"	27/4/16		Visited Div. H"rs also 149 Inf. Bdge. Fd. Co. at LOCRE, also C.E. at BAILLEUL.	

Army Form C. 2118

110

WAR DIARY
or
INTELLIGENCE SUMMARY
(Erase heading not required.)

Instructions regarding War Diaries and Intelligence Summaries are contained in F. S. Regs., Part II. and the Staff Manual respectively. Title Pages will be prepared in manuscript.

Place	Date	Hour	Summary of Events and Information	Remarks and references to Appendices
FLETRE	28/4/16		2nd North. Fd. Co. W.E. marched from LOCREHOF-FARM to Farms at Q.34.8. (Sheet 27). Visited 157 Inf. Bde. & 2nd North. Fd. Co. Visited 50. Div. H.Q. Gro.	
"	29/4/16		Inspected 7th Fd. Co. W.E. at training – visited 2nd North. Fd. Co. Visited C.R.E. 3rd Div., also 1st North. Fd. Co. & 7. D.Z.9. (Penviers) at LA CENTRE – Visited work in VIERSTRAAT SWITCH.	
"	30/4/16		Clears out for "Snipers" Rifle Range work by 9.10.3., Capt Anderson, & Assistant &c. Visited H.Q. 50. Div.	

A. Tupin Lt. Col. M
C. R.E. 50 Div

Original

War Diary
of
C. R.E. 50th Division

from 1st May 1916
to 31st May 1916

Army Form C. 2118

111.

WAR DIARY
or
INTELLIGENCE SUMMARY
(Erase heading not required.)

Instructions regarding War Diaries and Intelligence Summaries are contained in F.S. Regs., Part II. and the Staff Manual respectively. Title Pages will be prepared in manuscript.

Place	Date	Hour	Summary of Events and Information	Remarks and references to Appendices
FLÊTRE	1/5/16		C.R.E. went on short leave to U.K. Visited 2nd Fd. Dn. Hdqrs.	
"	2/5/16		Visited Lutting party at LOCRE and 1st Coy at LA CLYTTE	
"	3/5/16		2nd Fd. Coy. returned. 1st Fd. Co. on VIERSTRAAT SWITCH.	
"	4/5/16		2nd Coy. returned. 1st N. Fd. Co. and one arranged fields for chief manufacture, attendance demonstration of manufacture for attendance by Infantry.	
"	5/5/16		Visited 1st Fd. Co. LOCRE. C.E. V Corps – Corps Park	
"	6/5/16		150th Bde.	
"	7/5/16		LOCRE – C.E.V.Corps	
"	8/5/16		1st Fd. Co. – Lectures to Pioneers, attendance demonstration of fullerphone	
"	9/5/16		LOCRE. "	
"	10/5/16		Attended Lecture on Gas.	
"	11/5/16		Visited LOCRE – Lecture to Pioneers. 1st Coy returned and by 4th VIERSTRAAT SWITCH.	
"	12/5/16		C.R.E returned from leave – Visited 50th Div. H.Qr. & 7th Fd. Co. at LA CLYTTE.	
"	13/5/16		Attended Conference of Brigadiers at 50th Div. H.d. Qtrs. re work in future. Visited 2nd North Fd. Co.	
"	14/5/16		Visited C. Pt. 3rd Div. re manufacture of screens etc. thus CANADA CORNER, Dumps. Inspected VIERSTRAATSWITCH with O.C. 7th Co. R.E. – Visited C.E.5 Corps – Re packed Baileur. Visited 149th Inf. Bage. H.Qtrs. & saw M. Bungo. Interpreter as to purchase of camera. Visited 50 Div H.Qtrs. re attack orders.	

WAR DIARY
or
INTELLIGENCE SUMMARY

(Erase heading not required.)

Army Form C. 2118

112.

Place	Date	Hour	Summary of Events and Information	Remarks and references to Appendices
FLÊTRE	15/3/16.		Visited 50th Div. H'drs. re' attack orders. Inspected 1st North. Fd. Co. 2nd Lt. Co. Henderson D.S.O. re. O.C. Signal Co. 2nd Army called. Visited J.D.L.S. (Pioneers).	
"	16/3/16.		Visited C.E. 1st Anzacs. Major Bond R.E. is his Staff Officer. Later visited C.E. 5th Corps and J. Fd. Co R.E. at LA CLYTTE to arrange with re VIERSTRAAT SWITCH. Inspected huts under construction at LOCRE.	
"	17/3/16.		Drove to BOULOGNE with G.S.O.3, Capt. Anderson, & 2 M.A. Officers to inspect Army Works Section. Visited Lt. Col. Goodwin R.A.M.C.	
"	18/3/16.		Inspected 1st & 2nd North. Fd. Cos. - Visited 50th Div. H'drs. Attended 50th Div. Athletic Sports.	
"	19/3/16.		Inspected 1st North. Fd. Co. and J.D.L.S. (Pioneers). Visited C.E. 5th Corps, R.E. Park, CANADA CORNER, LOCRE HUTS, J. Fd. Co. R.E.	
"	20/3/16.		Visited G.O.C. 150 Inf. Bde. & 2nd North. Fd. Co. Visited G.O.C. 151 Inf. Bde.	

Army Form C. 2118

113

WAR DIARY
or
INTELLIGENCE SUMMARY
(Erase heading not required.)

Instructions regarding War Diaries and Intelligence Summaries are contained in F. S. Regs., Part II. and the Staff Manual respectively. Title Pages will be prepared in manuscript.

Place	Date	Hour	Summary of Events and Information	Remarks and references to Appendices
FLETRE	21/5/16.		7th Fd. Co. RE. marched from LA CLYTTE to Reat Billets or relief by 1st South. Fd. Co. RE. from work on VIERSTRAAT SWITCH. — inspected 7th F.C. on march. To KEMMEL with G.O.C. 150 Inf. Bdge. to select site for new Bdgr. Hd. Qrs.	
"	22/5/16.		To 50th Div. Hd. Qrs. about all arrangements for parade tomorrow for presentation of medals. Visited CAESTRE. To WESTOUTRE to see C. RE. 3rd Div. to inner. Visited Offic 5th Corps.	
"	23/5/16.		Attended Parade of 50th Div. before 2nd Army Commander, at which he presented medals. Visited this Corps.	
"	24/5/16.		Visited 50 Div. Hd. Qrs. re schemes + 2nd South. R.E. Inspected 1st South. F.C. at LA CLYTTE + turned out LOCRE, also G.O.C. 150 Inf. Bdge.	
"	25/5/16.		Visited 50th Div. Hd. Qrs. then saw G.O.C. 150 Inf. Bdge. Inspected 7th Fd. Co. RE.	
"	26/5/16		Visited 50th Div Hd. Qrs., then RE Park, STRAZEELE. Saw C. RE. 3rd Div. as to taking over + took over R.E Park, CANADA CORNER.	

Army Form C. 2118

WAR DIARY
or
INTELLIGENCE SUMMARY
(Erase heading not required.)

114.

Place	Date	Hour	Summary of Events and Information	Remarks and references to Appendices
WESTOUTRE.	27/5/16		Took over from C.R.E. 3rd Division. Spent morning with G.S.O.I. 50' Div. on Attack Scheme. G.H.Q. Coy. Vet. moved to M. #2.2. (Sheet 28) and 2nd Lines H.Q. to LOCREHOF FARM today.	
"	28/5/16		Visited 1st South M. Co., KEMMEL - DEFENCES, 2nd South M.Q. & G.O.C. 150 Inf. Bde., also 50' Div H9 Qrs. Inspected new water supply at foot of MONT ROUGE.	
"	29/5/16		Visited 150' H Co., 7' H Co., 250' Tunnelling Co. H2 & 135' A.T. Co. r r. Visited 50' Div. H9 Qrs + inspected area water supply near CANADA CORNER.	
"	30/5/16		Visited 2nd Army H9 Qrs + lunch with Major Hornold 4 per Prime Deminstration at Castets School, 3rd Army – Visited 50' Div H9 Qrs	
"	31/5/16		Inspected Div. Baths H9 Qrs on SCHERPENBERG. Visited 7' + 1st South M. Co. Inspected water supply + new Bdge. Hq Qrs at KEMMEL. Started night shifts on work at Mt. Noir.	

[signature]
F. Col. Mr.
C. R.E. 50' Div.

www.ingramcontent.com/pod-product-compliance
Lightning Source LLC
Chambersburg PA
CBHW081426160426
43193CB00013B/2201